MAKING OLD-TIME FOLK TOYS

Sharon Pierce

 Sterling Publishing Co., Inc.   New York

Other books by Sharon Pierce
Making Folk Toys and Weather Vanes
Making Whirligigs and Other Wind Toys

*For Karen and Tim, in memory of our
childhood and with thanks for our
friendship*

Edited by Katherine Balch
Photography by Elizabeth Matthews
Front cover photograph by Dick Frank
and Frank Attardi

Library of Congress Cataloging-in-Publication Data

Pierce, Sharon.
    Making old-time folk toys.

    Includes index.
    1. Wooden toy making.   I. Title.
TT174.5.W6P546   1986   745.592   86-6033
ISBN 0-8069-4780-2 (pbk.)

Copyright © 1986 by Sharon Pierce
Published by Sterling Publishing Co., Inc.
Two Park Avenue, New York, N.Y. 10016
Distributed in Canada by Oak Tree Press Ltd.
℅ Canadian Manda Group, P.O. Box 920, Station U
Toronto, Ontario, Canada M8Z 5P9
Distributed in the United Kingdom by Blandford Press
Link House, West Street, Poole, Dorset BH15 1LL,
England
Distributed in Australia by Capricorn Ltd.
P.O. Box 665, Lane Cove, NSW 2066
Manufactured in the United States of America

TABLE OF CONTENTS

EDITOR'S NOTE

Patterns for some of the toys are too large to reproduce in this book. They have been reduced, therefore, by 25% and printed on top of a ¾-in. grid. To enlarge these patterns so you can use the sizes of materials given in the directions, buy 1-in. grid paper or make your own. Draw a portion of the original pattern one square at a time. Make the line running through the 1-in. square correspond directly to the line running through the book's ¾-in. square. After enlarging the pattern in this way, cut it out and continue instructions for making the poster-board pattern.

METRIC CONVERSION CHART

Inches to Millimetres and Centimetres

inches	mm	cm	inches	cm	inches	cm
⅓	3	0.3	9	22.9	30	76.2
¼	6	0.6	10	25.4	31	78.7
⅜	10	1.0	11	27.9	32	81.3
½	13	1.3	12	30.5	33	83.8
⅝	16	1.6	13	33.0	34	86.4
¾	19	1.9	14	35.6	35	88.9
⅞	22	2.2	15	38.1	36	91.4
1	25	2.5	16	40.6	37	94.0
1¼	32	3.2	17	43.2	38	96.5
1½	38	3.8	18	45.7	39	99.1
1¾	44	4.4	19	48.3	40	101.6
2	51	5.1	20	50.8	41	104.1
2½	64	6.4	21	53.3	42	106.7
3	76	7.6	22	55.9	43	109.2
3½	89	8.9	23	58.4	44	111.8
4	102	10.2	24	61.0	45	114.3
4½	114	11.4	25	63.5	46	116.8
5	127	12.7	26	66.0	47	119.4
6	152	15.2	27	68.6	48	121.9
7	178	17.8	28	71.1	49	124.5
8	203	20.3	29	73.7	50	127.0

PREFACE

*A*s a maker and collector of toys, I am fascinated most by old toys, what I term heirloom toys, that can withstand frequent handling and still be passed on to another generation. This book was written and the toys designed with that delightful trait of longevity in mind. There is something special, almost sacred, about heirlooms that have been in one's family for decades. If cared for, the toys in this book should last many years so that they, too, can be passed on to future generations.

Several of the toy designs in this book employ unique methods of operation, such as the pendulum that makes the penguins rock on the seesaw, and the wooden weights for both the Indian and the tightrope walker that lower the figures' center of gravity. Not only will these toys provide amusement for children, they are also intriguing to adults.

Some of the other toys are extremely simple to make, for example, the spinners and blocks, but they will provide hours of playtime. A toy need not be complex to be enjoyed, as is proved over and over again when children successfully entertain themselves with cardboard boxes, paper, or string.

Since I do not believe in re-inventing the wheel, the designs for several projects include wooden items, such as drawer pulls and embroidery hoops, that can save you time.

None of the projects in this book is very difficult or time-consuming, although some may appear more difficult merely because they require more materials and take longer than others. Construction of these toys requires only a minimum of tools.

I suggest reading through the instructions before starting on any project. When choosing a project, keep in mind the age of the child you plan to give it to. Good judgment should be used when selecting any toy for a child under three, since they are prone to put everything in their mouths and chew on them.

These old-time toys are not only fun to give but fun to make. You may be tempted to make one for yourself, if only for display.

HISTORY OF TOYS

*E*ver since the beginning of civilization, children have probably amused themselves with some form of crude toy or game, perhaps pebbles or clay balls.

We do know that toys, since ancient times, have occupied an important part in the life of children. They provide fun while enabling the child to learn about the world. Children also learn how to get along with others and develop certain skills, such as eye and hand coordination.

Some of the earliest recorded playthings are simple clappers, rattles, and balls. This same assortment of toys has remained popular to this day, although the materials they are made from have improved with technology.

Children of ancient Greece are known to have played with toy carts, hobbyhorses, hoops, and kites, while children from ancient Egypt amused themselves with balls, pull toys, and carved animal figures. Balancing toys, usually carved entirely of wood, can be traced back to ancient China and India.

During medieval times, youngsters were provided with a wide array of toys, including toy soldiers. And although the ordinary child's toys were carved into a basic shape from bone or wood, the wealthy child's toys were often crafted from silver or bronze and made with fine, detailed workmanship.

As early as the 15th century, Germany became known as one of the best producers of quality toys, and Nuremberg became the leader in the manufacture of wood toys and wood carvings. It is also around this time that the earliest recorded toy cradles of European origin appeared.

By the 18th century, German toys could be found in England, America, Italy, and Russia, when many people were able to afford commercially produced toys for their children. Realistic-looking dolls, rocking horses, and puzzles—all became popular from this period on.

In the latter half of the 19th century, metal toys were increasing in popularity and wooden toys decreasing. Many of the metal toys were produced in Germany in both Württemberg and Nuremberg; these included detailed amusement rides, such as the Ferris wheel and merry-go-round. America at this time was also manufacturing metal toys, and especially important were those made from cast iron.

Most of the American "tin" toys—horse and wagons, boats, and so on—were made in New York, Connecticut, and Philadelphia, Pennsylvania, but it was not until after the Civil War that they were produced in great numbers.

Although table games such as checkers and chess have been popular since ancient times, it took until the end of the 19th century for manufacturers to start introducing new and unusual board games. Now, every year new games are introduced, many of them electronic, filling shelves of toy shops with a wide array to choose from.

Now that the toy industry has been bombarded with video and electronic toys, one might expect a lack of interest in ordinary wooden ones; however, with the current trend in back-to-basic living, there has been a surge of interest in wooden toys, particularly those resembling old-time toys.

TOYMAKING

The rewards of toymaking are many, whether you have chosen to make toys as a hobby or as a profession. Monetary compensation is irrelevant compared to the delight, smile, or hug of a young child when presented with a handmade toy made just for him. Adults, as the primary purchasers of toys, are also highly appreciative of the time and care invested in the making of a fine toy.

Making toys is one of the oldest hobbies and a most satisfying pastime. It is an extremely rewarding experience to start with a solid piece of wood and then, by your own hand, gradually turn it into a charming toy. Although it is exciting, working with your hands (and heart) is also therapeutic.

When we think of toymakers, two familiar characters come to mind—Geppetto, whose only puppet became Pinocchio (from the children's story *The Adventures of Pinocchio*); and Santa Claus, the most prolific of all toymakers. I don't think anyone would mind being compared to either craftsman.

Regardless of age, there will always be a little child in all of us. The toys in this book will make a handsome acquisition for any toy collector, and they will certainly delight and amuse the children in your life.

COLOR

*C*olor. This simple, yet amazing, finishing touch can make the difference between a masterpiece with visual appeal and a lifeless object. I am not referring to the use of only bright or bold colors; the color depends upon the object. For instance, can you imagine Leonardo da Vinci's Mona Lisa with bright-red hair and electric-blue clothing? This is a rather drastic example, but you get the point.

Selecting the right color can be time-consuming. Designers agonize over it. You can create a great design and ruin it with the wrong color.

Many toys are attractive simply left the color of their natural wood, but there is something exciting and wonderful about a colorful toy. It's obvious that children love bright objects from the first moment of sight. And although children seem perfectly happy with any color toy, I must admit that I spent more time deciding the color of the toys in this book than I did designing them.

In most instances, I have chosen rather muted shades of the primary colors. These were achieved by mixing a very small amount of black with either red, green, or blue. In the case of yellow, a small amount of dark brown was used.

Color is, of course, a matter of preference. You might want brighter colors or ones that blend with the color scheme of a room. So feel free to paint your toys differently from the way they are illustrated here. I made the seesaw project for one of my daughters and painted it pink and lavender, attaching coordinated ribbons around the penguins' necks, because these are her favorite colors.

So, for a more personal touch, especially when the toy will be displayed in the child's room, I suggest finding out the child's favorite colors and also the color of the room and accessories.

Generally, I prefer working with acrylic tube paints. They are quick-drying, and brushes can be washed with soap and

11

water. The colors are permanent when dry.

Before starting the projects in this book, you might want to purchase the basic colors. These same colors are used repeatedly throughout the book, and one tube of each should suffice:
titanium white
mars black
burnt umber
turner's yellow
naphthol red light
red oxide
cerulean blue hue
permanent green deep
hooker's green

Although there are many other tints close to these colors, these are my first choice.

GENERAL INSTRUCTIONS

*B*efore starting any project, read through the entire materials list and instructions. If you already have materials that can be substituted for those listed, then use them. I always try to use what I have instead of buying additional materials.

Where patterns are supplied, use transparent tracing paper for duplicating the pattern. Transfer this onto poster board—a thin, smooth cardboard—and cut around the outline. Afterwards, these poster-board patterns can be stored away for future projects.

Follow directions carefully to determine the correct thickness of wood required for each pattern piece. Most of the toys consist of more than one thickness of wood.

Although I usually choose pine for toys, you may prefer another softwood or one of the hardwoods.

Cutting can be done on either a scroll saw or band saw. Be sure to use a ⅛-in. blade if you make any intricate cuts. Take

special care not to injure yourself when cutting the small pieces required by some of the designs.

Most drilling can be done with a small portable drill, but for certain toys, such as the circus wagon and the zoo, I highly recommend a drill press. Not only does it ensure accurate drilling but it also saves time.

In most cases, sanding can be done entirely by hand. However, if you have a sander, you can save time by employing it for the majority of the sanding. Finishing, or final, sanding should be done by hand with a fine-grade sandpaper.

Each project includes detailed mixing instructions for painting. If you plan to make several of these old-time toys, I suggest consulting the paint list on page 12, and stocking up on the basic colors.

Always be sure to allow time for glue to set and dry before handling the project again. Also give ample time for paint and stain to dry before assembling the toys.

MATERIALS & EQUIPMENT

*T*his is a summary of the materials and equipment you will need to make the toys in this book. Some of the materials listed are used for only one or two of the projects; however, a description of the essential details is given.

Materials

WOOD
Most of the projects require ¾-in. pine or ⅜-in. pine. Occasionally, various thicknesses of plywood are needed. Choose a good quality, if possible, such as birch plywood. The difference in quality is worth the extra price.

WOODEN DOWELS
Various-sized dowels are used for many of the toys. When drilling holes for dowels, drill into scrap wood first and test the fit, since the diameters of dowels often vary from one to the next.

DRAWER PULLS
Manufactured in assorted sizes, these wooden balls come in handy as heads, weights, and so on.

FLAT WOOD TRIM
This flat trim, measuring ¼ x 1½ in., can be found in the lumberyard along with the mouldings. It is used for the farmyard and horse in the hoop.

WOODEN FINIALS
Pieces of wood that have been turned on a lathe make decorative accents for several projects, such as the merry-go-round. They are available from hardware dealers.

WOODEN QUILTING HOOPS, EMBROIDERY HOOPS
These hoops are sold as a pair—an inside hoop and an outside hoop. Usually only the solid inside hoop is used for these toys.

LAZY SUSAN APPARATUS
This is a ball-bearing device (Illus. 1) that enables the merry-go-round to spin. A manufactured lazy Susan may be purchased from a hardware dealer instead.

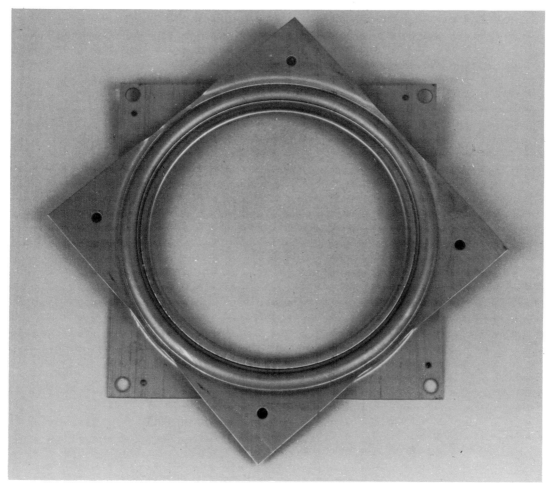

Illus. 1. This Lazy Susan device can be used for two of the projects in this book.

HINGE

Buy a long hinge in a strip that can be cut to desired lengths. This is used for the roof of the ark, so it can be opened and closed for animal storage.

BRASS RODS

These can be purchased at a hobby shop or hardware dealer. If unavailable, substitute any stiff wire and adjust drill-bit size accordingly.

COPPER WIRE

Use 14-gauge wire for connecting the jointed toys, such as the wooden doll. Needle-nose pliers are required for bending.

BLACK STEEL WIRE

Select a thin, stiff, 16-gauge wire. It is used for some toy joints and the Ferris wheel wires. Bend the wire with needle-nose pliers.

COTTER PINS
These split pins hold the wheels on the axle of toys such as the horse and wagon.

MUSLIN
An unbleached fabric, muslin is used in the construction of the feed and seed bags.

POLYESTER FIBRE STUFFING
This man-made fibre, often sold in hobby shops for stuffing pillows and animal shapes, is used here to fill the feed and seed bags.

SANDPAPER
Most sanding, whether by hand or machine, requires medium-grade paper. Final sanding should always be done by hand, with a fine-grade sandpaper.

PAINT
Many of the toys in the book require the application of acrylic tube paints. A complete listing of the colors that are used throughout the book can be found on page 12.

STAIN
Several of the toys need to be stained instead of painted. There are many types and colors of stain; choose a good-quality brand for best results.

BRUSHES
Use artist-quality brushes in ¼-in., ½-in., ¾-in., and 1-in. sizes.

WOOD GLUE
Yellow wood glue should be used for all projects requiring glue. Clamp or weight sections that have been glued for a strong, durable bond.

TRACING PAPER
Trace the patterns from this book with transparent paper.

POSTER BOARD
Make pattern templates with this thin cardboard, which is also known as oak tag.

Equipment

GOGGLES
Always wear some type of eye protection when cutting, sanding, or drilling.

DUST MASK
Although dust masks are recommended when sawing and sanding most woods, they are essential for some woods, such as mahogany and pressure-treated lumber.

TABLETOP SCROLL SAW
A scroll saw has a vibrating blade, and it is especially useful for small intricate work. Choose a fine-tooth blade. Some scroll saws have a sanding wheel, which can perform most sanding.

BAND SAW
A band saw has a thin, continuous blade. It can make intricate cuts or saw through a 4 × 4. Choose a ⅛-in. blade for intricate work and a ¼-in. blade for straight cuts.

SANDER

Use either a sanding wheel, as on the scroll saw, or a small stationary belt sander. Use medium-grade sandpaper.

DRILL

Any portable hand drill is suitable. A variety of drill bits are needed, including a 2¼-in.-diameter, circle-cutting bit.

DRILL PRESS

A stationary drilling machine that makes straight and accurate holes.

NEEDLE-NOSE PLIERS

These thin, tapered pliers can bend and cut wire.

Rolling Toys

Horse in Hoop

This is both a beautiful display piece and also a toy that is fun to roll around. The horse remains stationary—in his running position—while the hoop rolls (Illus. 2).

MATERIALS
Pine, ¾ in. thick: 8 × 12 in.
Wood trim (flat), ¼ × 1½ in.: 5 ft. long
Wooden dowel, ⁵⁄₁₆ in. diameter: 7 in. long
Quilting hoops, 14 in. diameter: two
Wooden beads, ⁵⁄₁₆-in.-diameter opening: two large, two small; or substitute ⅝-in.-diameter dowel: 6 in. long
Acrylic paint: cerulean blue hue, mars black, titanium white, burnt umber, naphthol red light
Brush: ½ in.
Wood glue
Sandpaper: medium and fine grades
Tracing paper
Poster board

Illus. 2.

TOOLS

Scroll saw or band saw
Drill with 5⁄16-in. and 21⁄64-in. bits

INSTRUCTIONS

Pattern. Trace the pattern (Illus. 4) for the horse and transfer it onto the poster board. Cut out this template and then trace onto the 3⁄4-in. pine.

Cutting. Using a scroll saw or band saw, cut out the figure of the horse. Cut two 13¾-in.-long pieces of the flat trim. Measure before cutting, to be sure this is just slightly larger than the inside diameter of the circular quilting hoop. If not, you will not get a snug fit when gluing.

Also, cut three 6½-in.-long pieces from the flat trim. Now, cut the 6½-in. strips in half lengthwise so that you have six strips 3⁄4 in. wide by 6½ in. long.

Next, cut a 7-in. length of the 5⁄16-in.-diameter dowel. If you do not have wooden beads, cut four ½-in. pieces from a 5⁄8-in.-diameter dowel.

From one of the remaining sections of quilting hoop, cut two 1¼-in. pieces. (Illus. 3). Cut these both in half lengthwise. These small curved pieces will be used as supports when gluing the long strips of trim (crosspieces) to the hoops.

Drilling. Find the balance point of the horse. Approximate point is marked on the pattern, but this should be checked for accuracy if your horse is to stay in an upright position. The horse should re-

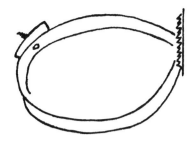

Illus. 3. Cutting the hoop

main in his balanced position while the hoop rolls, except for rocking to and fro a little.

The method I use to find the center of balance is to hold the horse lightly (from above) with my thumb and middle finger. If it is held lightly in different positions you will notice that the horse will either swing forward or backwards, or if perfectly balanced, it will remain upright (running position). If you can grasp the horse with your fingernails this is even better for determining the exact point to mark. Now, drill a 21⁄64-in. hole through the horse at this point.

Using the 5⁄16-in. bit, drill a hole through the middle of both 13¾-in. crosspieces. If you are using dowel pieces instead of beads, drill through the center of each of these.

Sanding. Sand all pieces and edges smooth using medium-grade sandpaper. Edges of the horse may be sanded round with either an electric sander or by hand.

Round the ends of the long crosspieces to fit into the curve of the hoop.

Give all pieces a final sanding by hand with a fine-grade sandpaper.

Illus. 4. Pattern for Horse in Hoop

Painting. Paint pieces as follows. All measurements are approximate.

Horse, outside beads: ½ tsp. red / ½ tsp. burnt umber

Remaining pieces (except dowel, which is left its natural color): 1 tsp. blue / ¼ tsp. white / ¼ tsp. black

Assembling. Insert dowel through the horse and then position two large beads on either side of the horse. These should be placed next to the horse but not against it.

Glue a crosspiece to each hoop, making sure they are positioned at the widest points of the hoop. At this time you will also be gluing the small curved supports to the hoop adjacent to the crosspiece (Illus. 5). Let this dry.

Now, slide each end of the dowel into a crosspiece. Let about ¼ in. extend through the outside for the bead. Glue the 6½-in. support strips in place, one on either side of each crosspiece, and one halfway between each crosspiece. (See Illus. 2.)

Let this dry well. Your horse is now ready for his first race!

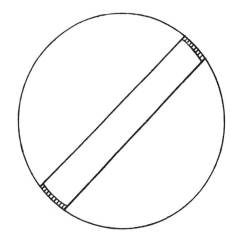

Illus. 5. Gluing a crosspiece

Circus Wagon

Everyone loves the circus, and any boy or girl will fall in love with this circus toy (Illus. 6). Be ambitious and make a train of circus wagons, each a different color.

MATERIALS

Pine, ¾ in. thick: 5 × 8 in.
Pine, ⅜ in. thick: 10 × 15 in.
Birch plywood, ¼ in. thick: 3 × 6 in.
Wooden dowel, ³⁄₁₆ in. diameter: 12 ft. long

Wooden dowel, ¾ in. diameter: 4 in. long
Copper wire, 14 gauge: 1 ft. long
Cotter pins, ³⁄₆₄ × ½: four
   or black steel wire, 16 gauge: 1 ft. long
Acrylic paint: turner's yellow, naphthol red light, titanium white, mars black
Brushes: ¼ in. and ½ in.
Wood glue
Natural-color jute: 2 ft. long
Sandpaper: medium and fine grades
Tracing paper
Poster board

TOOLS

Scroll saw or band saw
Stationary belt sander or sanding wheel

Illus. 6.

Drill with 1⁄16-in., 5⁄64-in., 3⁄16-in., and 13⁄64-in. bits
Circle-cutting bit, 2¼-in. diameter
Needle-nose pliers

INSTRUCTIONS

Pattern. Trace the pattern pieces and transfer them onto poster board. Cut out these templates and then trace the tiger, two of each elephant leg, two wagon-top patterns, and four axle supports onto the ⅜-in. wood. Also draw one wagon base 3¼ × 8⅞ in., two strips ⅜ × 8⅞ in., and two strips ⅜ × 2¼ in.

Onto the ¾-in. wood, trace the elephant body. Then, onto the ¼-in. board trace two ears and also draw two strips ⅜ × 2¼ in.

Cutting. Cut out all of the above pieces with the scroll saw or band saw. Then cut thirty 4¼-in. lengths of the 3⁄16-in. dowel. Also cut two dowels 4¾ in. long for the axles. Cut a 4-in. length of ¾-in. dowel.

Drilling. Using the 1⁄16-in. bit, drill a hole through each of the 4¾ in. dowels, about ⅛ in. from the end (Illus. 8). Drill a 5⁄64-

Illus. 7. Patterns for Circus Wagon

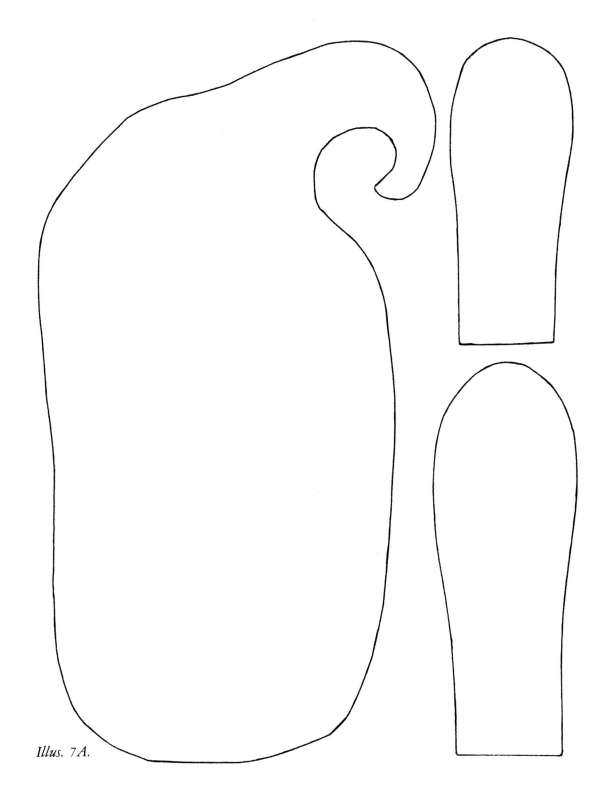

Illus. 7A.

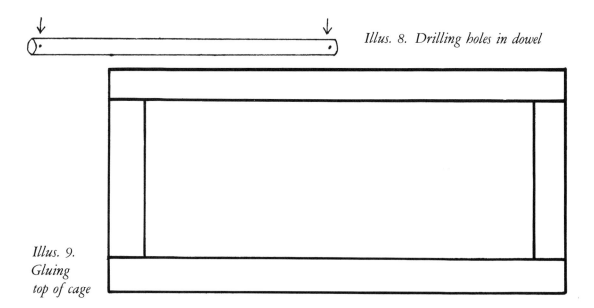

Illus. 8. Drilling holes in dowel

Illus. 9.
Gluing
top of cage

in. hole into the elephant (for the tail) and two holes, ¼ in. deep, into the underside of the base, 1 in. apart, center front.

Before drilling the holes for the bars of the cage, first glue the ⅜-in. strips together to form the top of the cage (Illus. 9). When this is dry, position it on top of the base piece. Mark holes to be drilled, approximately ½ in. apart and ¼ in. from the edge. There should be twelve holes on each side, with three additional holes across the ends. Drill these with the ³⁄₁₆-in. bit, through the top section and ¼ in. into the base. If you drill two opposite corners first and then put a short scrap of dowel into these holes, it will keep all holes aligned perfectly. If possible, use a drill press.

From the ⅜-in. wood, cut four wheels using the 2¼-in. circle-cutting bit. Drill center of wheels with a ¹³⁄₆₄-in. bit.

Sanding. Use the sander to sand the large cage parts and also the elephant and wheels. Give all pieces a final sanding by hand with a fine-grade sandpaper.

Gluing. Glue the 4¼-in.-long "bars" into the base and also into the top of the cage. Press dowels in evenly and snugly. Glue the side ornamental tops in place. The ¼-in.-thick strips, 2¼ in. long, should be glued to the front and back of the top, between the ornamental tops.

Glue the elephant's legs and ears in position. Be sure feet are flat and level. When the cage is dry, turn it upside down and glue the axle supports flush with the sides about ¾ in. from each end.

Painting. Paint the elephant and cage as follows. Remember that measurements are approximate.
Wheels: ½ tsp. yellow

Cage: 1 tsp. yellow/ 1 tsp. red
Elephant: ½ tsp. black / ½ tsp. white
Tiger: 1/4 tsp. yellow / few drops of
red / black stripes
Eyes: dot of white / smaller dot of black
on top of white

Assembling. Slide dowels through axle
supports, add wheels, and insert cotter
pins or cut four 1¼-in.-long pieces of
steel wire. Loop ends with needle-nose pliers.

Cut a 7-in. length of the 14-gauge copper
wire. Bend the middle of this loosely
around a pencil and then twist the wires
three times. Spread the ends apart and
bend the last ½ in. upwards (Illus. 10).

Illus. 10. Bending the wire

Glue these into the holes that have already been drilled underneath the front of
the cage.

Then cut a 4½-in. piece of copper wire.
Bend it into a long **S**-shape for a tail. Cut
a piece of jute about 1½ to 2 ft. long.
Twist this around the wire, gluing as you
go. Glue the tail into the elephant. The
tail makes a hook for pulling the circus
wagon (cage).

Slide the ¾-in.-dowel piece through the
elephant's trunk, and he's ready to work.

Horse & Wagon

Little children will love loading and un-
loading the feed and seed wagon. The
horse can pull the wagon, and to make it
even more mobile, you could add a base
with wheels for the horse. This is a favorite of mine, and it's sure to be a favorite
of any toy fancier.

MATERIALS
Pine, ¾ in. thick: 5 × 8 in.
Pine, ⅜ in. thick: 10 × 12 in.
Birch plywood, ¼ in. thick: 4 × 6 in.
Wooden dowel, ³⁄₁₆ in. diameter: 3 ft. long
Cotter pins, ⁵⁄₆₄ × ½: four
    or black steel wire, 16 gauge: 1 ft.long
Muslin, unbleached: ¼ yd.
White thread and a needle
Permanent black marker: fine point
Natural-color jute: 1 ft. long
Polyfill stuffing: one handful
Acrylic paint: red oxide, titanium white,
burnt umber, turner's yellow, permanent
green deep, mars black
Brushes: ½ in. and ¼ in.
Stain: light oak
Wood glue
Sandpaper: medium and fine grades
Tracing paper
Poster board

TOOLS
Scroll saw or band saw
Stationary belt sander or sanding wheel

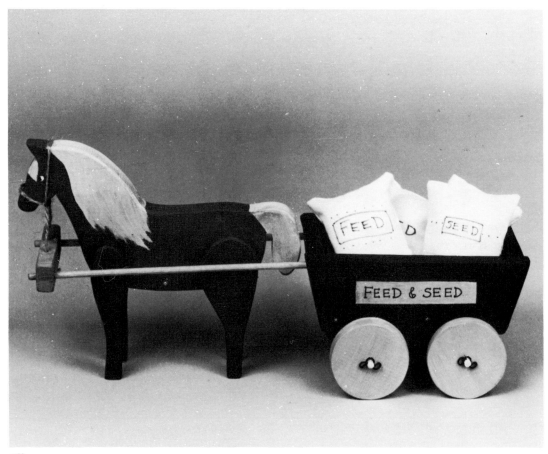

Illus. 11.

Circle-cutting bit, 2¼-in. diameter
Drill with ¹⁄₁₆-in., ⅛-in., ³⁄₁₆-in., and ¹³⁄₆₄-in. bits
Needle-nose pliers

INSTRUCTIONS

Pattern. Trace all pattern pieces and transfer onto poster board. Cut out these templates and then trace the horse's body onto the ¾-in. wood. Trace two of each leg, two wagon sides, and four axle supports onto the ⅜-in. wood. Also draw two pieces, 2⅛ × 3 in. on the ⅜-in. wood, for the wagon's front and back. Leave room for four 2¼ in. wheels that will be cut with the drill later.

Cutting. Cut out the above pieces using either a scroll saw or band saw. Cut off the bottom edges of the 2⅛ × 3-in. pieces at a 14° angle so that they will fit flush with the bottom. Now, cut a ¾ × 3-in. piece of ⅜-in. wood. This will serve as the front harness.

From the ¼-in. wood, cut a 3¾ × 4¾-in. piece for the wagon bottom. Then, cut a ½ × 2¾-in. piece from the ¼-in. scrap as an inside support for the harness poles.

Dowels should be cut accordingly: two, 5⅜ in. long, and two, 8½ in. long.

Drilling. Using the 3⁄16-in. bit, drill two corresponding holes into both the harness and the wagon front approximately 2⅛ in. apart (Illus. 12). Holes should be about ¼ in. from the top of the wagon front. Also drill corresponding holes into the ¼-in. inside support piece. Use this same bit to drill a hole through the center of each axle support piece.

Drill two ⅛-in. holes into the top of the harness piece, approximately ¾ in. apart (Illus. 13).

With the 2¼-in. circle-cutting bit, cut four wheels from the remaining ⅜-in. wood. Then drill 13⁄64-in. holes through the middle of each wheel. Drill a 1⁄16-in. hole ⅛ in. from each end of the 5⅜-in. dowels in order to accommodate the cotter pin or wire.

Sanding. Sand all pieces, including wheels, with the sander. Round the edges. Give each piece a final sanding by hand, with a fine-grade paper.

Gluing. Glue the horse's legs in place, making sure the feet are flat and level. Glue the wagon sides to the front and

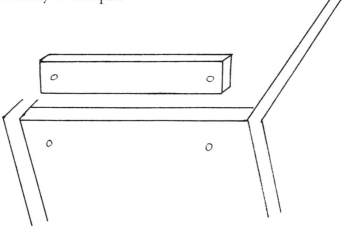

Illus. 12. Points for drilling holes into wagon and into the support piece

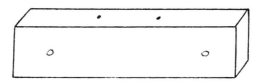

Illus. 13. Points for drilling harness

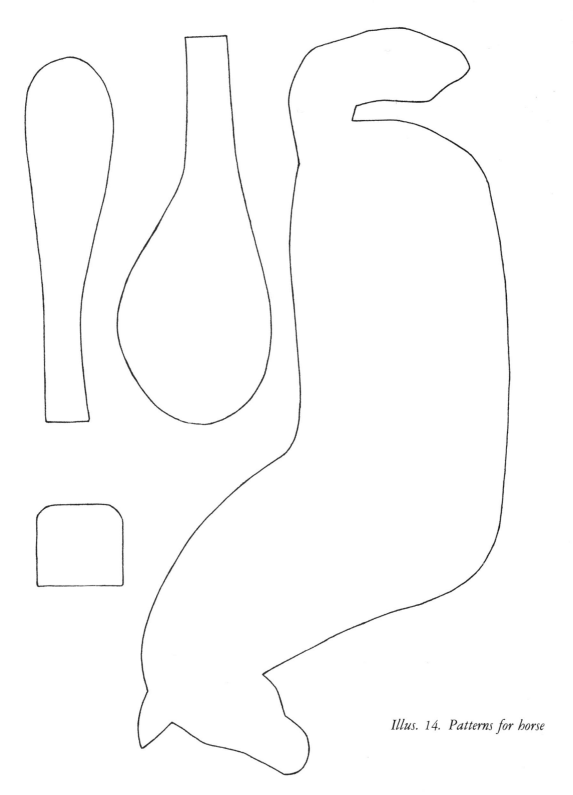

Illus. 14. Patterns for horse

Illus. A1. The Merry-Go-Round.

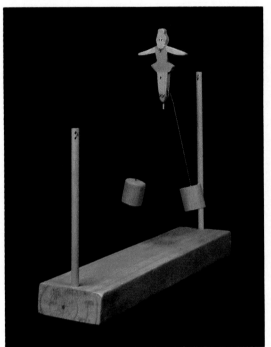

Illus. B1. Tightrope Walker.

Illus. B2. Ring-Around-a-Rosy.

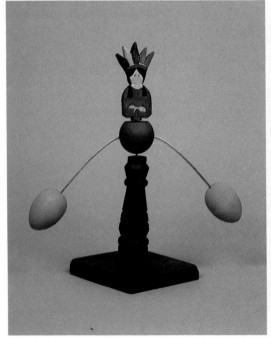

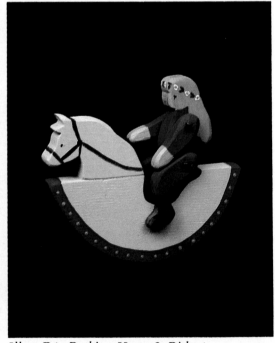

Illus. B3. Balancing Indian.

Illus. B4. Rocking Horse & Rider.

Illus. C1. Blocks and Houses.

Illus. C2. Horse & Wagon.

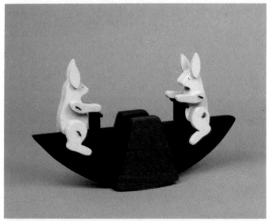

Illus. C3. Rocking Rabbits.

Illus. C4. Zoo and Animals.

Illus. C5. Doll Cradle.

Illus. C6. Circus Wagon.

C

Illus. D1. Ferris Wheel.

Illus. D2. Wagon.

Illus. D3. Checkerboard & Checkers.

D

Illus. 15. Pattern for wagon

back pieces. When dry, turn the wagon upside down and glue the bottom in place. Also glue the axle supports to the bottom, approximately ½ to ¾ in. from the front and back.

Painting. Paint the horse and wagon with the following colors. Measurements are approximate.
Horse mane, tail: ½ tsp. white / drop of burnt umber
Horse body: 1 tsp. red
Wheels, sign: 1 tsp. yellow / drop of burnt umber
Wagon: 1 tsp. green / drop of black
Eyes: dot of white / smaller dot of black on top of white

Write FEED & SEED on sign with a black, permanent marker. Stain harness and dowels with a light oak stain.

Sewing. Feed and seed bags are made by cutting four 3¼ × 8-in. pieces of unbleached muslin. Fold in half lengthwise and then stitch a ⅜-in. seam on each side, either by machine or by hand, leaving an opening 1½ in. long on one side. Trim the seam to ¼ in., turn the piece right side out, and then stuff it loosely with polyfill. Close the opening with hand stitches (Illus. 16). Use the black marker to label bags FEED and SEED.

Assembling. Insert the short axle dowels through the supports and slide a wheel on either side. Secure with either cotter pins or steel wire looped at each end with needle-nose pliers.

Cut a piece of jute 12 in. long. Tie this

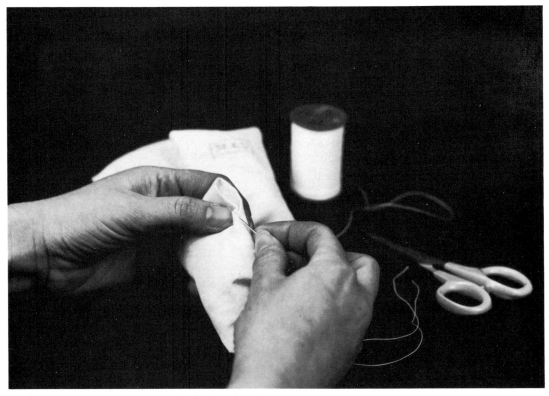

Illus. 16. Leave one seam on the feed and seed bags open so that you can stuff the bag. Then close it by hand.

behind the horse's ears and around his nose. Knot it underneath his chin. Slide each end of the jute through the ⅛-in. holes of the harness and then knot it underneath.

Slide the long dowels into the harness (¼ in. extending in front) and then, with the horse in position, insert the other ends into the wagon. Glue the ¼-in. support piece to the dowels and to inside of wagon front.

Fill with feed and seed bags, and this horse is ready for his first delivery.

Noah's Ark

On Sundays in the 19th century, many children were forbidden to play boisterously, but toys such as this one were not only allowed but popular. There is something special about the animals parading into the ark two by two. This rendition serves as storage for the animals and can also be rolled around during play. Add a string, and it's a pull toy.

Illus. 17.

MATERIALS

Pine, ¾ in. thick: 11 × 22 in.
Birch plywood, ¼ in. thick: 14 × 24 in.
Wooden dowel, ⁵⁄₁₆ in. diameter: 1 ft. long
Hinge: 11¾ in. long
Flat wood screws, ¼ x 4: twelve (or
number required by the hinge)
Cotter pins, ³⁄₆₄ × ½: four
  or black steel wire, 16 gauge: 6 in. long
Acrylic paint: turner's yellow, burnt
umber, naphthol red light, cerulean blue
hue, mars black
Brushes: ¼ in. and 1 in.
Wood glue
Sandpaper: medium and fine grades
Tracing paper
Poster board

TOOLS

Band saw
Drill with ¹⁄₁₆-in., ⁵⁄₁₆-in., and ¹¹⁄₃₂-in. bits
Circle-cutting bit, 2¼ in. (for wheels)
Needle-nose pliers
Screwdriver

INSTRUCTIONS

Pattern. Trace the pattern piece (Illus.
18) and transfer it onto poster board. Cut
this out and then trace two of these onto
the ¼-in. wood. Also draw two 4¼ × 11-
in. pieces (for the sides) and two 3½ ×
11¾-in. pieces (for the roof) on the ¼-
in. wood.

Draw the base piece onto ¾-in. wood ac-

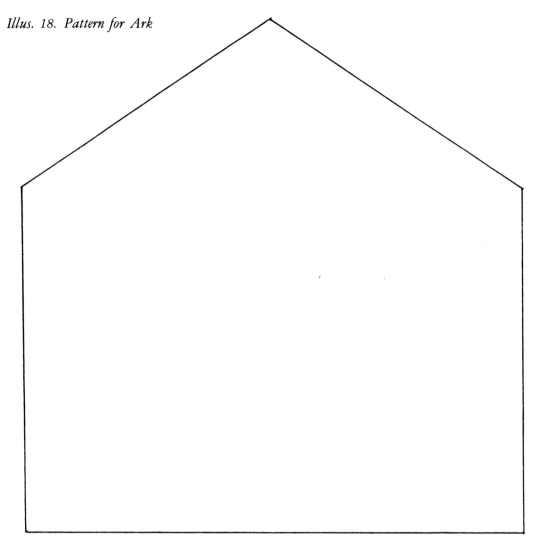

Illus. 18. Pattern for Ark

cording to measurements given in Illus. 19. Also draw two 1¾ × 2½-in. pieces and two 1 × 3 in. pieces. You will need two axle pieces ¾ × 8 in. Be sure to leave room to cut out four 2¼-in.-diameter wheels with the circle-cutting bit.

Cutting. Cut out all above pieces with the band saw. Also cut a 1⅜ × 9-in. ramp from the ¼-in. wood. Cut seven thin strips ¼ × 1⅜ in. for the ramp rails

(see Illus. 17). From the ⁵⁄₁₆-in. dowel, cut four 1¾-in. pieces.

Set the table part of your saw to cut a 25° angle. Now, trim the two 1 × 3-in. miniroof pieces—once lengthwise and then on both sides (Illus. 20, 21).

Drilling. Cut out four wheels with the wheel-cutting bit. Then drill the middle of the wheels with an ¹¹⁄₃₂-in. bit. Use the

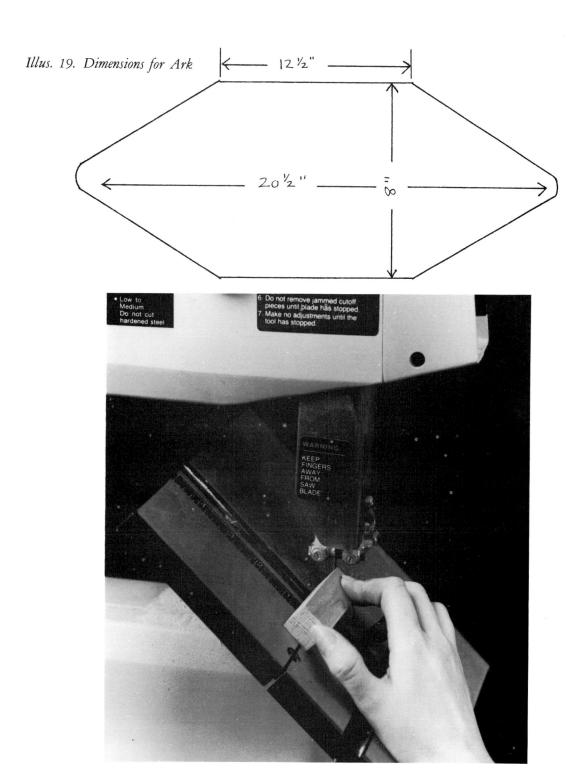

Illus. 19. Dimensions for Ark

12 ½"

20 ½"

8"

Illus. 20. Cutting the miniroof pieces at an angle

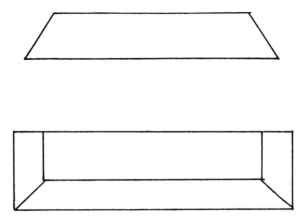

Illus. 21. Diagram of miniroof

⁵⁄₁₆-in. bit to drill into the end of each axle piece. Drill ¹⁄₁₆-in. holes into the side of each dowel approximately ⅛ in. from each end.

Sanding. Sand all pieces with a medium-grade sandpaper and then give a final sanding with fine-grade paper.

Assembling. Glue the axle pieces to the underside of the base and then glue the house part of the ark onto the base. Glue the doorways and miniroofs to the front and back of the house section, making sure they are centered. Set this aside to dry. Now, screw the hinge to the underside of the two roof sections. Glue the step strips to the ramp, approximately 1 inch apart. Paint before attaching the wheels.

Painting. Paint the ark with the mixtures given. Measurements are approximate.
House: 2 tsp. yellow / 1 tsp. white / ¼ tsp. burnt umber
Wheels, miniroof: 1 tsp. blue / ¼ tsp. black / ¼ tsp. white
Base, axles, roof: 1½ tsp. burnt umber / 1½ tsp. red
Stencil or paint windows with above paint mixture.

Finishing. Glue the dowels into the axle holes and then slide on the wheels. Secure with cotter pins or black steel wire. (Cut four 1¼-in. pieces. Curve ends with needle-nose pliers.)

The ark may be used to simply roll around, or if you'd like to make a pull toy, drill a hole in the front of the base and add a thin rope. Knot both ends.

Your ark is now ready for occupancy!

Illus. 22.

Ark Animals

Whether you make an ark or not, these little pairs of animals will provide hours of playtime.

MATERIALS
Pine, ⅜ in. thick: 11 × 14 in.
Acrylic paint: titanium white, mars black, burnt umber, turner's yellow, naphthol red light, hooker's green
Brush: ¼ in.
Sandpaper: medium and fine grades

Tracing paper
Poster board

TOOLS
Scroll saw or band saw

INSTRUCTIONS

Pattern. Trace each animal pattern and transfer them onto poster board. Cut out each of these and then trace two of each onto the pine board.

Cutting. Cut out the animals, being especially careful not to injure yourself when cutting the smaller animals.

Illus. 23. Patterns for Ark Animals

Illus. 24.

Sanding. Sand each animal with medium-grade sandpaper. Finish sanding with a fine paper.

Painting. Paint the ark animals with the following colors. Remember that measurements are approximate, so you might have to add a small amount of one color or the other.

Ducks, horse mane: ¼ tsp. white / drop of burnt umber

Kangaroos: ¼ tsp. white / ¹⁄₁₆ tsp. burnt umber

Hippos: ¼ tsp. white / ⅛ tsp. burnt umber

Horses: ¼ tsp. white / ¼ tsp. burnt umber

Rabbits, elephants: ½ tsp. white / ¼ tsp. black

Rhinos: ¼ tsp. white / ¼ tsp. black

Camels: ¼ tsp. yellow / ⅛ tsp. burnt umber

Alligators: ½ tsp. green

Lions, giraffes: 1 tsp. yellow / drop of red / drop of burnt umber

Lion mane, giraffe spots: ¼ tsp. burnt umber

Eyes: dot of white / dot of black on top of white dot

The animals are now ready for their journey!

Spinning Toys

Illus. 25.

Spinners

Spinners are very simple toys to make but are challenging for children because they have to do something to make the toy move. And once they start the toy spinning, they usually can't resist repeating the fun over and over again.

MATERIALS

Small Spinner
Wooden ball, 2 in. diameter (drawer pull)
Wooden ball, 1 in. diameter (drawer pull)
Wooden dowel, 7/8 in. diameter: 7/8 in. long

Wood glue
Acrylic paint: turner's yellow, naphthol red light, cerulean blue hue
Brush: 1/2 in.
Sandpaper: medium and fine grades

Large Spinner
Wooden ball, 3 1/4 in. diameter (finial)
Wooden ball, 1 in. diameter (drawer pull)
Wooden dowel, 1 1/4 in. diameter: 1 1/2 in. long
Wood glue
Acrylic paint: red, turner's yellow, permanent green deep
Brush: 1/2 in.
Sandpaper: medium and fine grades

TOOLS

Band saw

INSTRUCTIONS

Cutting. Cut dowels to appropriate lengths. Then cut the wooden ball in half using the band saw. To cut, hold the ball firmly with the aid of two blocks of wood, one on either side. (Since you are using a drawer pull or finial, you will have one flat surface to keep the ball more secure.) Cut slowly and carefully, or the ball might start to spin.

Sanding. Sand all pieces by hand with medium and then fine sandpaper. All edges should be rounded slightly. This extra little step always seems to make a toy look more inviting than when the edges are square.

Painting. Listed below are the approximate proportions of paint used.

Small Spinner
Ball: ⅛ tsp. yellow
Curved base: ¼ tsp. red
Dowel, flat base section: ¼ tsp. blue

Large Spinner
Ball: ⅛ tsp. red
Curved base: ½ tsp. green
Dowel, flat base section: ½ tsp. yellow

These are very colorful when spinning, especially if three different colors have been applied. Any combination of bright colors would be effective.

Assembling. Glue the dowel on top of the base. Then glue the ball on top of the dowel. Let these dry for a day before using. It is hard to resist spinning these simple little toys, but it will be worth the wait.

Ring-Around-a-Rosy

A colorful, mesmerizing toy that will delight any youngster. Twist the large circle as far as it will go and set these little people in motion, first spinning one way and then the other.

MATERIALS

Pine, ¾ in. thick: 10 × 26 in.
Pine, ⅜ in. thick: 6 × 20 in.
Wooden finial, 1¼ in. diameter
Wooden dowel, ⅜ in. diameter: 10¾ in. long
Twine: 8 ft. long
Acrylic paint: titanium white, naphthol red light, turner's yellow, permanent green deep, cerulean blue hue, mars black
Brush: ½ in.
Wood glue
Sandpaper: medium and fine grades
Tracing paper
Poster board

TOOLS

Scroll saw or band saw
Drill with ⅛-in., ⅜-in., and ¹⁵⁄₃₂-in. bits
Sander (optional)

INSTRUCTIONS

Pattern. Trace the pattern for the people and then transfer this onto poster board. Cut out and you now have a reusable template. On the ¾-in. wood, draw a 9½-in. circle and two 7-in. circles. Draw

Illus. 26. Pattern for figures

two 2½-in. circles and six people on the ⅜-in. wood.

Cutting. Cut out the pieces you have just drawn and then cut a 10¾-in. length of the ⅜-in. dowel.

Drilling. Using the ⅜-in. bit, drill a hole through the middle of the 2½-in. circles. Drill approximately three fourths of the way through the middle of the 7-in. circles. Use the ¹⁵⁄₃₂-in. bit to drill through the middle of the large 9½-in. circle. Glue a 2½-in. circle to each 7-in. circle, aligning the holes.

Now, mark four sets of double holes (Illus. 27) approximately ¾ in. from the

middle hole of the 9½-in. circle and also on *one* of the 7-in. circles to which you have already attached a 2½-in. circle. Using the ⅛-in. bit, drill the eight holes

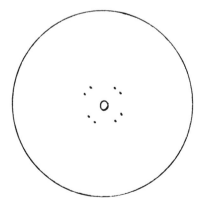

Illus. 27. Marking of drill holes

Illus. 28.

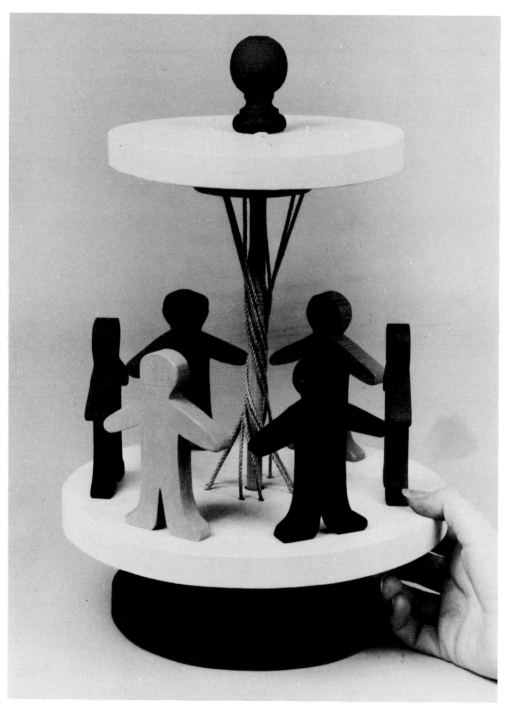

Illus 29. Turn the large circle so that the ropes twist around the central dowel.

into these three circles. These will house the twine.

Sanding. Sand all pieces either with a sander or sand well by hand using medium-grade sandpaper. Finish sanding with fine-grade paper.

Painting. There are many possibilities for paint combinations with this toy. You may choose a two or three-tone color combination, such as pink and lavender or red, white, and blue.

The colors given here are the same as those in Color Illus. B2. Measurements are approximate.
Large circle, top circle: 1½ tsp. white
Base circle, finial: 1 tsp. red / drop of black
People (¼ tsp. each): one, yellow; one, red; one, blue; one, orange (half yellow / half red); one, green; one, light green (half green / half white)

Assembling. Cut four 24-in. lengths of twine. Glue the dowel into the base circle. Slip the large circle onto the dowel and then glue the top circle in place. Also glue the finial on top at this time. Thread the twine through the drilled holes of the top and through the bottom. Tie underneath. The middle circle should hang about an inch above the base. Be sure this circle is level, adjusting the string as necessary.

Now glue the little people around the outer edge of the swinging circle. When dry, twist the large circle around a couple of times and then watch "Ring-Around-a-Rosy!" (See Illus. 29.)

The Merry-Go-Round

What child, or even adult, doesn't love the merry-go-round? This easy-to-make version is a working toy. It operates with a ball-bearing, lazy Susan apparatus. Just watching it spin is very entertaining.

MATERIALS
Pine, ⅜ in. thick: 10 × 14 in.
Plywood, ¾ in. thick: 16 × 24 in. (two base circles) or substitute a manufactured lazy Susan
Lazy Susan apparatus, 4–6 in. diameter (omit if using a manufactured lazy Susan)
Sheet-metal screws, No. 6: eight
Wooden dowel, ⅜ in. diameter: 36 in. long
Wooden dowel, ⁵⁄₁₆ in. diameter: 28 in. long
Wooden dowel, ⅞ in. diameter: 24 in. long
Rust-colored felt: ¾ yd.
Rust-colored thread
Wooden finial

Wooden quilting hoop, 14 in. diameter
Acrylic paint: titanium white, mars black, burnt umber, turner's yellow, naphthol red light, cerulean blue hue, permanent green deep, red oxide
Brushes: ¼ in. and ½ in.

Illus. 30. Patterns for the horse and the lion

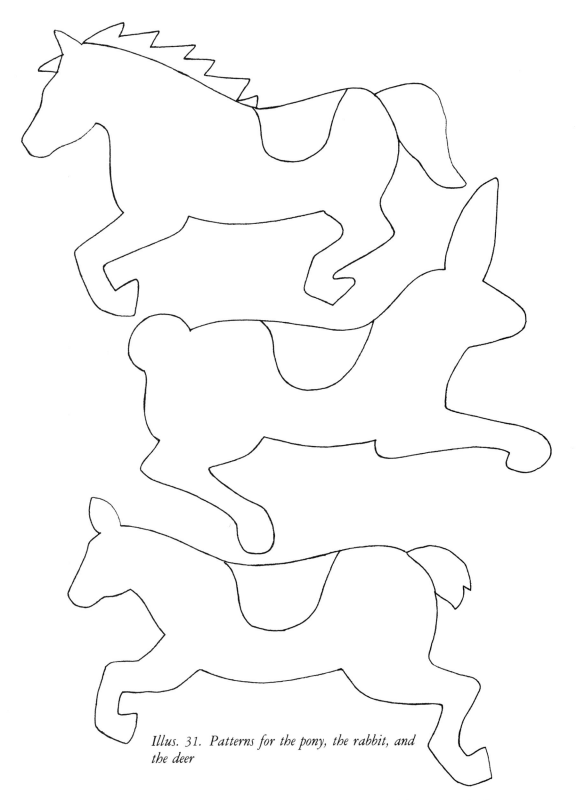

Illus. 31. Patterns for the pony, the rabbit, and the deer

Wood glue
Sandpaper: medium and fine grades
Tracing paper
Poster board

TOOLS

Scroll saw or band saw
Drill with ⅜6-in., ⅜-in., ⅝-in., and ⅞-in. bits
Screwdriver
Sewing machine (optional)

INSTRUCTIONS

Pattern. Trace pattern pieces and transfer onto poster board. Cut out templates, cutting around outlines only. Trace one deer, one horse, two ponies, two lions, and two rabbits onto the ⅜-in. wood. If you are making your own revolving base, draw two circles onto the ¾-in. plywood; one measuring 7 in. in diameter, the other, 15 in. in diameter.

Cutting. Cut the above pieces with either a scroll saw or band saw. Also cut four 8½-in. lengths of ⅜-in.-diameter dowel. Cut four 3-in. and four 4-in. lengths of the ⅜6-in.-diameter dowel. From the ⅞-in. dowel, cut one 13½-in. length and sixteen ⅜6-in. slices for decoration. Cut four small scraps measuring ¼ × ¾ in. of ⅜-in. wood. These will be glued to the hoop for stability, where the hoop and dowels join.

Drilling. Drill a ⅞-in. hole into the center of the 15-in. circle (or top of the lazy Susan), which will become the base for the merry-go-round. This hole should be about three fourths as deep as the wood is thick.

Center the hoop on top of the large circle. Make four equidistant marks on the 15-in. circle to indicate where holes should be drilled. These should be flush against where the hoop rests (Illus. 33) so that the dowels that will be glued to the base and the hoop will align. Drill these holes with the ⅜-in. bit.

Next, drill two staggered holes, indicated by **x**'s in Illus. 33, between the holes you just drilled. Use the ⅜6-in. bit for these.

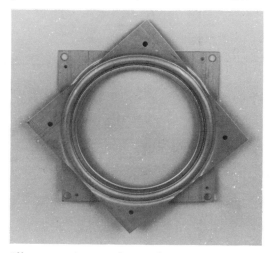

Illus. 32. A manufactured Lazy Susan apparatus

If you are making the revolving base, first center the lazy Susan apparatus on the 7-in. circle. Be sure the holes on the bottom piece that rests against the wood have a narrower diameter than the holes on the upper section. Screw the bottom piece to the circle. Turn the top piece, as shown in Illus. 34, and mark the screw opening on the 7-in. circle in one spot (equidistant from two attached screws). Drill a ⅜-in. hole through the 7-in. circle.

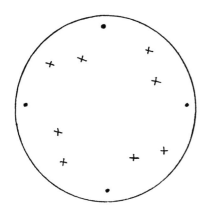

Illus. 33. Marking the drill holes

This will enable you to screw the 15-in. circle to the apparatus from the bottom.

Sanding. Using medium-grade sandpaper, sand all edges well. If a nice rounded edge is desired for the merry-go-round base, use a router. Give all pieces a final sanding by hand, with a fine-grade paper.

Painting. Paint the merry-go-round and animals with the following paint mixtures. Remember that measurements are approximate, and you might need to make slight adjustments to achieve the exact color you desire.

Rabbits, deer tail, pony and horse mane and tail: 1 tsp. white / drop of burnt umber

Deer: ¼ tsp. white / ¼ tsp. burnt umber

Lions: ¼ tsp. yellow / ⅛ tsp. burnt umber

Pony 1: burnt umber

Pony 2, horse: 1 tsp. black

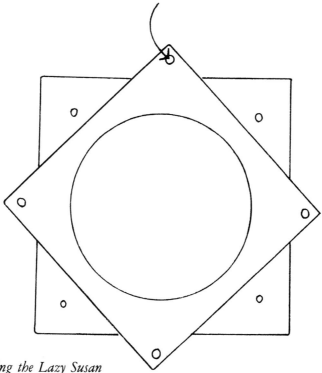

Illus. 34. Assembling the Lazy Susan

Illus. 35.

Lion mane and tail, center post: ½ tsp. red oxide

Base, rabbit saddles, finial, 8 dowel slices: 2 tsp. blue / ¼ tsp. white / ¼ tsp. black

Support dowels, saddles, pony 2, horse, 8 dowel slices: 2 tsp. yellow

Saddles, deer, pony 1: ¼ tsp. green

Saddles, lions: ¼ tsp. naphthol red light

Eyes: white dot / smaller black dot on top of white dot

Paint dots of red oxide around circumference of circle, as shown in Color Illus. A1.

Sewing. First, cut a circle from the rust-colored felt, with a 9½-in. radius (half the width). To do this, fold the fabric in half and then fold in half again, so that you have four thicknesses of material. Make sure all edges are even. Take a ruler and measure 9½ in. from the corner where all four thicknesses meet (Illus. 36). Make several measurements. Cut along the marks you've made, and this will produce a nice even circle.

Now, either by hand or by machine, sew four darts equidistant from one another,

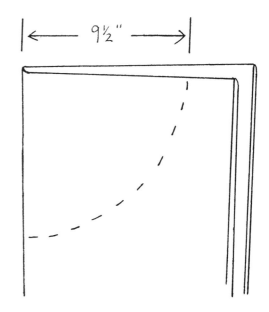

Illus. 36. Drawing the circle on felt

tapering from 1½ in. at the outside edge to nothing at the center of the circle (Illus. 37).

Assembling. If you have not already attached the 15-in. base circle, screw it onto the lazy Susan. Glue the center post in position and also the four support dowels.

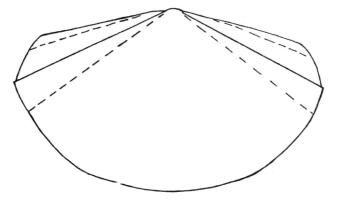

Illus. 37. Marking the fabric for taking in darts

Glue the tiny rectangles to the inside top edge of the hoop, where they will be supported by the dowels. Then glue the dowels to both hoop and rectangle (Illus. 38).

Merry-go-round animals can now be glued onto the ³/₁₆-in. dowels. Remember to alternate 3-in. and 4-in. dowels. Glue the dowels into the base.

Position the felt canopy. When centered, glue top to center dowel and then glue finial on top. Glue the sides to the hoop at only four spots, equally spaced, between each support dowel. Then glue alternating blue and yellow dowel decorations to the felt at these spots. Use a fair amount of glue, since it is absorbed by the felt.

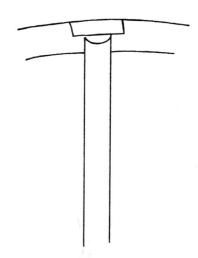

Illus. 38. Gluing dowel to hoop

The merry-go-round is quite attractive in motion, and it spins quietly and smoothly as you can now see for yourself!

Balancing Toys

Balancing Indian

This intriguing toy will provide hours of fun and amazement, as the Indian tips and spins without falling. It illustrates the principle that if the center of gravity of an object is below its point of support, it cannot be overturned. This is a toy that will delight both children and adults, and it makes a unique conversation piece.

MATERIALS

Pine, ¾ in. thick: 6 × 9 in.
Wooden drawer pull, 2 in. diameter
Wooden eggs, 2½ in. long: two;
   or wooden blocks, 1½ × 1½ in.: two
Turned chair leg: 6 in. long
   or similar wooden support
Wooden dowel, ⅛ in. diameter: 2 in. long
Brass rod, ³⁄₃₂ in. diameter: 12 in. long
Acrylic paint: red oxide, permanent green deep, turner's yellow, mars black, cerulean blue hue, burnt umber
Brushes: ¼ in. and ½ in.
Wood glue
Sandpaper: medium and fine grades
Tracing paper
Poster board

TOOLS

Scroll saw or band saw
Drill with ³⁄₃₂-in. and ⅛-in. bits
Sander (optional)
Woodcarving tools: ¼-in. flat chisel; small, all-purpose carving knife (optional)
Small C-clamp (G cramp) (if carving the Indian)

INSTRUCTIONS

Pattern. Trace the pattern (Illus. 44) for the Indian and transfer it onto poster board. Cut out the template, cutting around the outline only. This will give you a good pattern to use now and to save for additional use later. Trace the Indian onto the wood.

Cutting. Using the scroll saw or band saw, cut out the Indian body. Also cut out a 5-square-in. base piece from the ¾-in. pine. If you are not using the wooden eggs, you will need to cut two blocks of wood approximately 1½ in. square or use two round balls 1½–2 in. in diameter. Whatever objects you use, be sure they weigh exactly the same.

Also cut two 1-in. lengths of ⅛-in.-diameter dowel. These will be used to attach the Indian to the drawer pull and to insert into the bottom of the drawer pull. This little point of the dowel is your Indian's balancing point.

If the surface on the top of the chair leg or post is not flat, cut a ¼-in. slice of ⅞-in. wooden dowel.

Drilling. Drill a ⅛-in. hole into the center bottom of the Indian and into both the center of the flat side of the drawer pull and into the center of its bottom (Illus. 40).

With the ³⁄₃₂-in. bit, drill a hole into a center point of each egg (or object used for weight). Then drill a hole into the side of the drawer pull, being careful to drill straight through the center and out the other side.

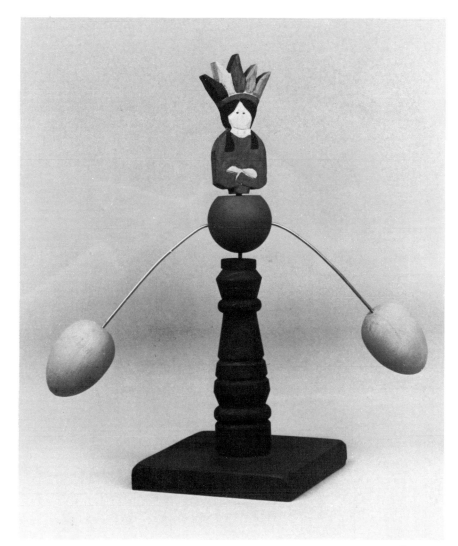

Illus. 39.

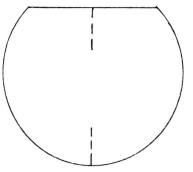

Illus. 40. Drilling positions on the drawer pull

Carving. Draw onto the wood the details of the Indian as depicted on the pattern. Round all edges and feather tips with the carving knife. Then clamp down the Indian and carve the details using the flat chisel. Be sure to keep your hands behind the blade at all times.

First define entire detail by pressing the chisel straight into the wood about ⅛ in.

Illus. 41. Carving tools

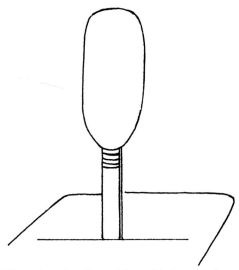

Illus. 42. Carving with a chisel: straight cut

Illus. 43. Carving with a chisel: angled cut

deep (Illus. 42). Do this in a continuous line. Then go over all details again by placing the chisel 1/16 in. from the incised line (chisel should be held at a 45° angle, as shown in Illus. 43) and then pressing into the wood to meet the first cut. Continue around the design.

If you have never done any carving before, practice on some scrap wood. Be sure to clamp your work piece down and keep your hands *behind* the blade.

Sanding. If you did not carve the details, be sure to sand all edges round. Whichever procedure you use, give a final sanding by hand with fine sandpaper.

Painting. Paint the Indian and base using the following mixtures of paints. Remember, measurements are approximate.
Chair leg and base: 1½ tsp. green / drop of black
Eggs (or equivalent): ½ tsp. yellow / drop of burnt umber
Indian suit, headband, middle feather, ball: ¾ tsp. red
Indian hair, eyes: ⅛ tsp. black
Remaining feathers: one, blue; one, yellow; one, dark green; one, light green (mix half yellow, half green)

Assembling. Glue the base and chair leg together and set aside to dry. Connect Indian to the drawer pull using the 1-in. length of dowel and glue. Also glue the other 1-in. dowel into the bottom hole of the drawer pull.

When dry, insert and glue the brass rod into the ball part of the Indian and center

Illus. 44. Pattern for Indian

it so that there is 5 in. of rod on either side of the ball. Bend both wires down equally, at about a 45° angle from the ball. Immediately insert and glue the wooden weights on each end. Before the glue dries, set the Indian on the chair leg base and make sure he is balanced. If not, move the wires little by little until the Indian is perfectly balanced. Leave it in this position to dry.

This clever Indian can now be tipped and spun, and he will not fall off the base.

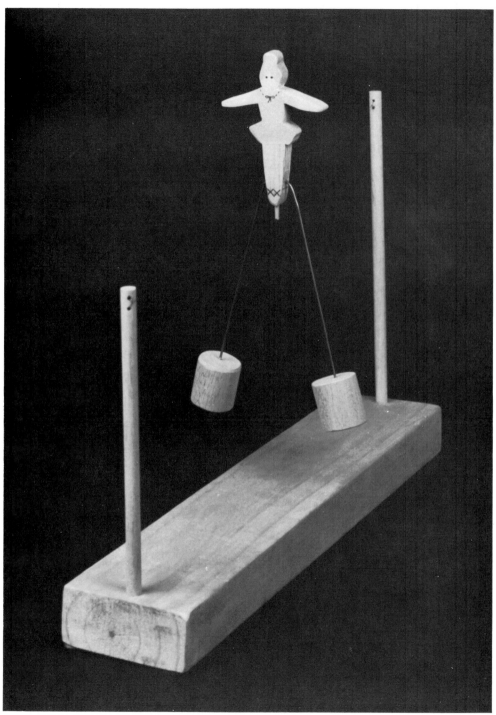

Illus. 45.

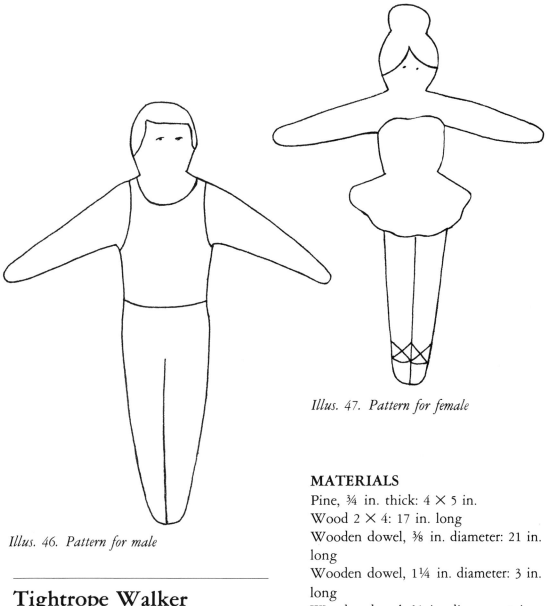

Illus. 47. Pattern for female

Illus. 46. Pattern for male

Tightrope Walker

Both children and adults will marvel at this tightrope walker's unfailing balance. Patterns are provided for either a man or a woman figure (Illus. 46 and 47). This makes a nice display piece.

MATERIALS

Pine, ¾ in. thick: 4 × 5 in.
Wood 2 × 4: 17 in. long
Wooden dowel, ⅜ in. diameter: 21 in. long
Wooden dowel, 1¼ in. diameter: 3 in. long
Wooden dowel, ⅛ in. diameter: 1 in. long
Brass rod, ³⁄₃₂ in. diameter: 12 in. long
Buttonhole thread or 16-gauge wire: 22 in. long
Acrylic paint: turner's yellow, titanium white, naphthol red light

Brushes: ¼ in. and ½ in.
Wood glue
Sandpaper: medium and fine grades
Tracing paper
Poster board

TOOLS

Band saw
Drill with ¹⁄₁₆-in., ³⁄₃₂-in., ⅛-in., and ⅜-in.
bits
Stationary belt sander or sanding wheel

INSTRUCTIONS

Pattern. Trace the pattern for the tight-rope walker and transfer it onto poster board. Cut out around the outline. Trace your poster-board pattern onto the ⅜-in. wood.

Cutting. Cut out the tightrope walker and then cut a 17-in. length of 2 × 4 for the base. Cut two lengths of ⅜-in.-diameter dowel: one, 8½ in., the other 12 in. Next, cut two 1¼-in. lengths of 1¼-in.-diameter dowel. Cut a 1-in. piece of ⅛-in. dowel.

Drilling. Using the ⅜-in. bit, drill two holes into the top side (at both ends) of the 2 × 4 base (three-fourths thickness of wood). Holes should be approximately ½ in. from the ends. Drill a ⅛-in.-diameter hole into the bottom of the feet of the tightrope walker.

With the ³⁄₃₂-in. bit, drill a hole into the middle of each 1¼-in. dowel piece. Now drill a hole through the side of the tight-rope walker's legs as indicated in Illus. 48. Finally, using the ¹⁄₁₆-in. bit, drill two

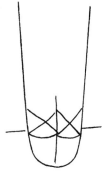

Illus. 48. Drilling position for holes at the feet

Illus. 49. Placement of holes in dowel

Illus. 50. V-shaped notch in dowel

holes through the top of each ⅜ in. dowel approximately ½ in. from the top (Illus. 49).

Sanding. Round all edges with the sander and then give a final sanding, by hand, with fine sandpaper. Sand a V-shaped notch in one end of the ⅛-in. dowel (Illus. 50). This is the only part that rests on the string.

Painting. Paint pieces with the colors listed below. Measurements are approximate.
Base, ⅜ in. dowels, hair: 2 tsp. yellow

Clothing, 1¼ in. dowels: ½ tsp.
white / ¼ tsp. red
Eyes: dot of black inside larger dot of
white

Assembling. Insert and glue ⅜ in.-
dowels into base. Tie thread onto dowels
through the drilled holes. To make the
thread taut, twist the dowels as much as
necessary. If desired, use 16 gauge wire instead of thread.

Insert and glue the brass rod through the
feet of the tightrope walker, centering the
figure on the rod. Bend the wires down as
shown in Illus. 45 and then glue the 1¼-
in.-dowel pieces to the ends.

Glue the ⅛-in. dowel into the bottom of
the feet (notched end down), check for
balance, and adjust wires accordingly. The
tightrope walker should stand in an upright position.

When dry, place your tightrope walker at
the highest end, and she will glide down
the rope on her own.

Creative Playtoys

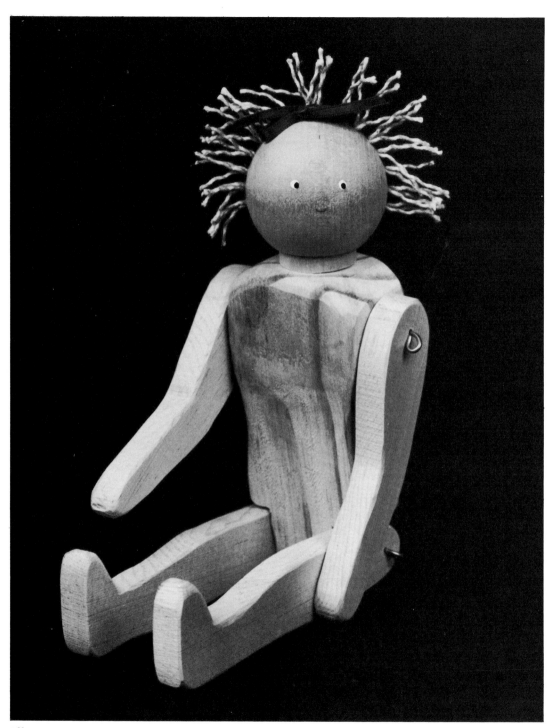

Illus. 51.

Jointed Wooden Doll

This plain wooden doll has a most unusual personality. Present her as is, or sew or paint some clothes for her. She is simple enough to be loved!

MATERIALS

Pine, ⅜ in. thick: 6 × 8 in.
Wood 2 × 4: 5 in. long
Round wooden ball (drawer pull): 2 in. diameter
Wooden dowel, 1¼ in. diameter: ¼-in. slice
Natural-colored twine: 1 yard
Ribbon, ¼ in. wide: 8 in long
Copper wire, 14 gauge: 1 ft. long
Flathead (countersink) wood screw, 1¼ × 12: one
Acrylic paint: titanium white, mars black (for eyes, optional)
Wood glue
Sandpaper: medium and fine grades

Tracing paper
Poster board

TOOLS

Band saw
Drill with ³⁄₃₂-in., ³⁄₁₆-in., and ¹³⁄₃₂-in. bits
Stationary belt sander or sanding wheel
Needle-nose pliers
Screwdriver

INSTRUCTIONS

Pattern. Trace all three pattern pieces and transfer them onto poster board. Cut out the patterns and then trace two arm and two leg pattern pieces onto the ⅜-in. wood. Trace the torso onto the 2 × 4.

Cutting. Cut out all pieces with the band saw. Taper the lower half of the torso by laying this piece on its side and cutting ¼ in. inward from the front bottom, tapering to the existing waistline (Illus. 53). Repeat this same cut on the back portion.

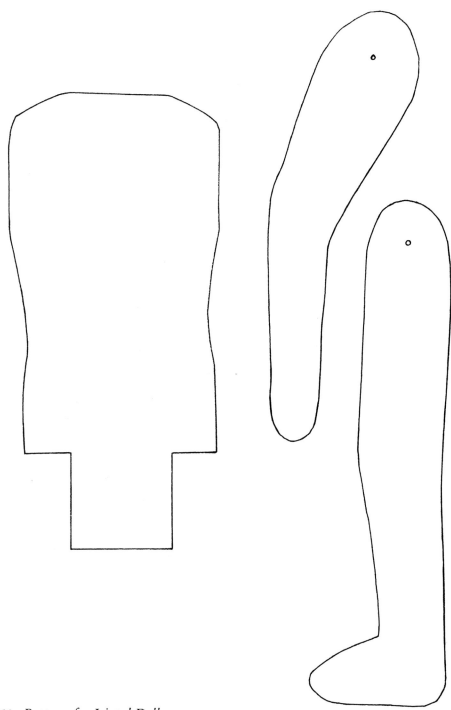

Illus. 52. Patterns for Jointed Doll

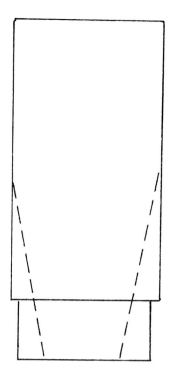

Illus. 53. Angles for tapering doll's body

Cut a ¼-in. slice from a 1¼-in.-diameter dowel. This will be used for the neck. If the wooden ball you are using for a head is not flat on one end, as the drawer pulls are, sand or cut a ¼-in. slice from one side.

Drilling. Drill a hole into the arms and legs, as indicated on the pattern, using the 3⁄32-in. bit. Drill corresponding holes into the torso. With this same bit, drill sixteen holes, approximately 3⁄8 in. apart into the wooden ball for the doll's hair. These holes start at about where one ear might be and continue across the top of the head to the other side as far down as where her other ear might be. If you pre-

fer a different hair treatment, such as yarn pigtails or painted hair, delete this last step.

Using the 3⁄16-in. bit, drill through the middle of the neck dowel. If you are not using a drawer pull, you will need to drill a short distance into the bottom of the head. Make sure the screw will be able to grip the wood. Countersink the neck hole, using a 13⁄32-in. bit to house the head of the wood screw. This will enable the head to move back and forth after the neck is glued to the torso.

Sanding. Round all edges with the sander. If a carved appearance is desired, round the edges more. Finish sanding, by hand, using a fine-grade sandpaper. Remember to sand with the grain of the wood to avoid scratches.

Assembling. The doll may be left the wood's natural color, or you can stain it with a light oak stain. Another variation would be to paint clothing onto the doll, such as a one-piece bodysuit with straps across the shoulders.

Screw the neck onto the head and then glue the neck to the torso. Be sure not to glue the screw or else the head won't be able to move back and forth. While this is drying, cut a 3½-in. piece and a 4¼-in. piece of copper wire with the pliers.

Using the pliers, curve one end of each wire into a small oval so that the end meets the wire (Illus. 53A). Insert the smaller wire into the leg, through the torso and through the other leg. Curve

Illus. 53A. Bending end of wire into oval

the other end. Use the other wire for the arms. Make sure the arms and legs are flush with the body but loose enough to move.

Now, cut sixteen 2-in. pieces of twine and glue one into each hole in the head. If twine resists going into the holes, put a small drop of glue on one end and let dry before trying to push it into the hole. When this has dried, unravel ends of the twine to give a fuller appearance. Tie a ribbon around the middle sections of hair.

Finish with the eyes by painting a small dot of white paint and then, when dry, apply a small dot of black paint inside the white dot. If you prefer, draw an eye with a black marker.

Ferris Wheel

A popular amusement-park ride, the Ferris wheel has entranced girls and boys for decades. This model really works and is just the right size for tiny bears and dolls. A classic toy for both children and collectors.

MATERIALS
Pine, ¾ in. thick: 11 × 15 in.
Birch plywood, ¼ in. thick: 8 × 16 in.
Wooden dowel, ⁵⁄₁₆ in. diameter: 5 ft. long
Wooden dowel, ³⁄₁₆ in. diameter: 1 ft. long
Wooden embroidery hoops, 10 in. diameter: two
Wooden beads, ⁵⁄₁₆-in.-diameter opening: two, or make beads from ⅝-in.-diameter dowel
Wooden drawer pull, 1 in. diameter (for handle)
Black steel wire, 16 gauge: 5 ft. long
Acrylic paint: turner's yellow, naphthol red light, cerulean blue hue, permanent green deep, mars black, burnt umber
Brush: ½ in.
Stain: light oak color
Wood glue
Sandpaper: medium and fine grades
Tracing paper
Poster board

TOOLS
Scroll saw or band saw
Drill with ³⁄₃₂-in., ³⁄₁₆-in., ⁵⁄₁₆-in., and ¹¹⁄₃₂-in. bits
Needle-nose pliers

INSTRUCTIONS

Pattern. Trace the Ferris-wheel chair pattern and the support patterns. Transfer these to poster board and cut out. On the ¾-in. wood, draw cutting lines for a 5 × 11½ in. base, and two 2-in.-diameter circles. Trace two tall supports and eight little chair supports.

Trace the chair pattern onto the ¼-in. wood eight times and then draw four backs that measure 1¾ × 2¼ in., and four seats that measure 1¾ × 1½ in. Also draw a piece ¾ × 2½ in. (round the ends) for the handle.

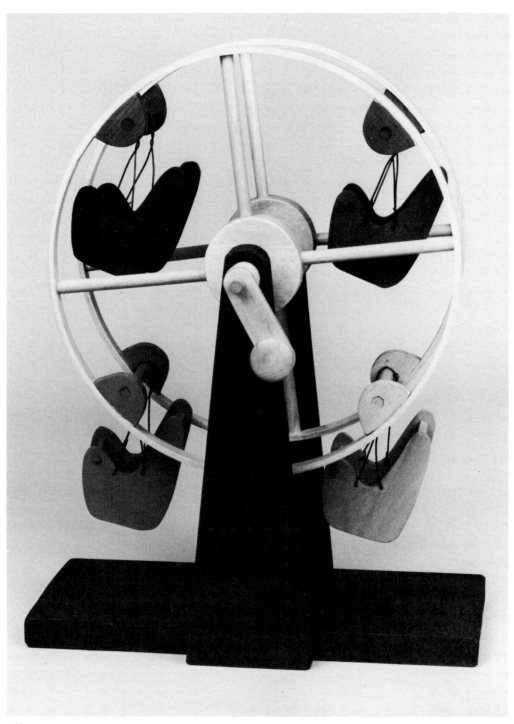

Illus. 54.

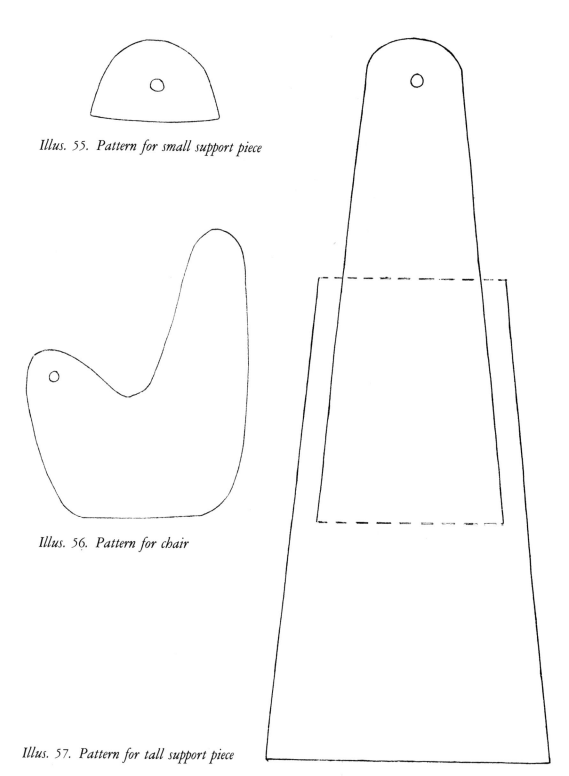

Illus. 55. Pattern for small support piece

Illus. 56. Pattern for chair

Illus. 57. Pattern for tall support piece

Cutting. Cut out all pieces with either the scroll saw or band saw. Also, from the ⁵⁄₁₆-in. dowel, cut twelve 4-in. pieces and one 8½-in. piece. From the ³⁄₁₆-in. dowel, cut four 2½-in. pieces.

Drilling. With a ⁵⁄₁₆-in. bit, drill a hole into the middle of all eight chair supports. Also, drill a hole into the middle of both 2-in. circles and into one end of the 2½-in. handle piece. Then drill four holes, equidistant from one another (Illus. 58) approximately ¼ in. deep into the rim of the circles.

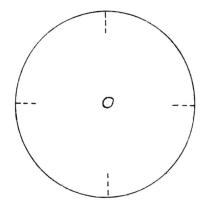

Illus. 58. Points at which holes should be drilled into circle

Use the ¹¹⁄₃₂-in. bit to drill through the tall support pieces as indicated on the pattern. Now, drill ³⁄₃₂-in. holes in each chair side for the wires and use a ³⁄₁₆-in. bit to drill holes into the chair sides for the safety bar (Illus. 59).

Sanding. Sand all pieces by hand using a medium-grade sandpaper. Finish sanding with the fine-grade paper.

Staining. Using a light oak color, stain the hoops, 2-in. circles, eight 4-in. dowels, center dowel, beads and handle. Let dry.

Gluing. Glue the tall supports to the base, centering them on each side. Be sure the holes at the top line up correctly. Glue the Ferris-wheel chairs together and insert the dowel safety bars. Set these aside to dry before painting.

Painting. Paint the remaining pieces accordingly. Measurements are approximate. Base, two tall supports: 2 tsp. green / drop of black

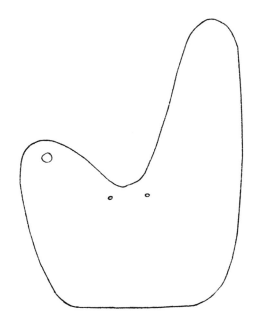

Illus. 59. Positions for drilling holes into chair

Chair 1, two supports, one dowel: ¾ tsp. red / drop of black
Chair 2, two supports, one dowel: ¾ tsp. yellow / drop of burnt umber

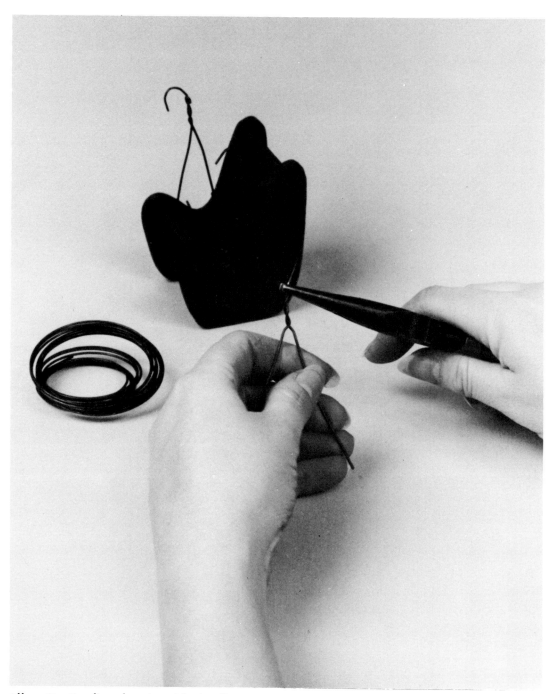

*Illus. 60. Bending the wire with the pliers to pro-
duce a hook so that the chair can hang on the
dowel*

Chair 3, two supports, one dowel: ¾ tsp. blue / drop of black
Chair 4, two supports, one dowel: ¾ tsp. green / drop of black

Assembling. Glue four stained dowels into each 2-in. circle. Glue the ends of the dowels to the inside of the hoops. Let dry. Now glue the colored chair supports into the center of each hoop quadrant as shown in Illus. 54. Make sure colors and also holes of both hoops correspond.

When this has dried properly, insert and glue the color-coordinated dowels into the supports. Slide the large dowel through the first base support, through the middle of both wheels and through the second base support. Leave ½ in. of the dowel extending from the first support and glue a bead onto the dowel. Do not get glue on the support or the wheel will not be able to move.

When you are sure the Ferris wheel is properly aligned, glue it into place (2-in. circles glued to dowel only). Now glue a wooden bead on the other end of the dowel, making sure once again that you do not glue the base support to anything. Glue the 2½-in. handle to the wooden bead as you slip it onto the dowel. At the other end of the handle, glue the drawer pull in place. The Ferris wheel should now operate smoothly.

The last step is to attach the wires to the Ferris wheel chairs. (An option here would be to use string in place of wires.)

Cut eight wires 3⅛ in. long and eight wires 3¾ in. long. Take a wire of each length and stand them, end down, on a table. At the point where the short wire ends, grasp both wires with the needle-nose pliers and twist the two wires around each other about three times.

Curve the top single wire so that it will hang on the corresponding dowel (Illus. 60). Bend the bottom ½ in. of each wire so that it will slide into the side of the chair (Illus. 61). Curve the ends around to meet the wires. Repeat this on each side of all Ferris wheel chairs. Make adjustments in bends and so on, so that the chair hangs level and straight.

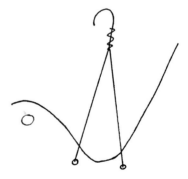

Illus. 61. Inserting wire into the chair

When all chairs are finished, hang them on the wheel, and then you're ready for a test ride. For extra fun, make little "people" with 1-in. dowels and 1-in. drawer-pull heads. Paint them bright colors or stain them.

Illus. 62.

Farmyard & Animals

This is a delightful piece that can be used either as a farmyard complete with farm animals, or as a Christmas yard at the base of a small tree.

FARMYARD:

MATERIALS

Plywood, ½ in. thick: 16 × 16 in.
Wood trim (flat) ¼ × 1½ in.: 12 ft. long

Acrylic paint: titanium white, burnt umber, hooker's green
Brushes: ½ in. and ¾ in.
Wood glue
Sandpaper: medium and fine grades

TOOL
Band saw

INSTRUCTIONS

Cutting. Cut a 16 × 16 in. piece of ½-in.-thick plywood for the base. Then cut twenty-four 3¾-in. lengths of the flat trim. Also, cut two 15½ in. strips. Cut all of the flat trim pieces in half lengthwise (strips should now be ¾ in. wide). Cut one end of each 3¾-in. piece into a dull point as shown in the pattern.

Sanding. Sand all pieces well, taking care to sand the points of the pickets. Make sure points are very dull.

Assembling. Lay twelve pickets on your work surface with an equal amount of space between them. Distance from the outer edge of the first one to the outer edge of the last one should be approximately 15½ in. Glue a 15½-in. strip to these about one inch from the top of the pickets (Illus. 63). Repeat with the remaining three sections. Let these dry.

Painting. Paint the base green. You will need about 3 to 4 teaspoons of paint.

Paint the fence sections white mixed with a few drops of burnt umber. This will produce an off-white. Approximately 4 to 5 teaspoons of paint will be needed for all fence sections.

Assembling. When all sections are completely dry, glue them to the base. Be sure the fence is level with the bottom of the base.

FARM ANIMALS:

MATERIALS
Pine, ¾ in. thick: 8 × 11 in.
Pine, ⅜ in. thick: 5 × 7 in.
Birch plywood, ¼ in. thick: (trough) 5 × 5 in.

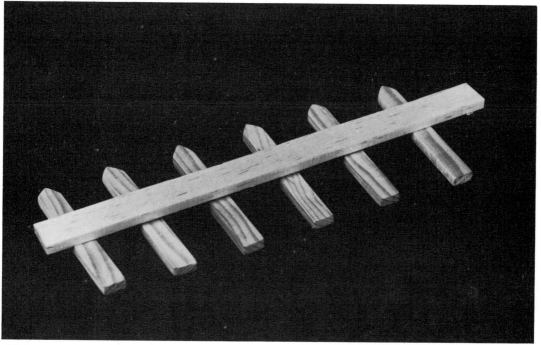

Illus. 63. Gluing fence sections

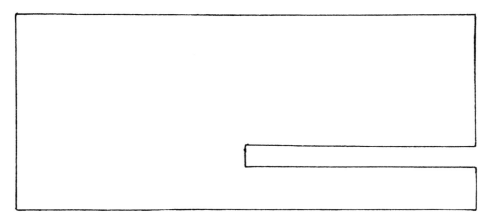

Illus. 64. Pattern for trough piece

Illus. 65. Pattern for picket

Acrylic paint: titanium white, mars black, burnt umber
Brushes: ¼ in. and ½ in.
Sandpaper: medium and fine grades
Tracing paper
Poster board

TOOL
Scroll saw or band saw

INSTRUCTIONS

Pattern. Trace pattern pieces and transfer onto poster board. Cut out templates around outlines only. Trace mother animals onto the ¾-in. wood and trace baby animals onto the ⅜-in. wood. Trace two trough pieces onto the ¼-in. wood.

Cutting. Cut out all pieces using either a scroll saw or band saw.

Sanding. Sand each piece with the medium-grade sandpaper. Then give a final sanding by hand with the fine-grade paper.

Painting. Paint the animals as shown. Colors are not mixed.
Cows: half black / half white
Pigs: half burnt umber / half white
Sheep: White / black accents
Trough: watered-down burnt umber

When dry, slide both trough parts together. Add a little straw or some pine needles.

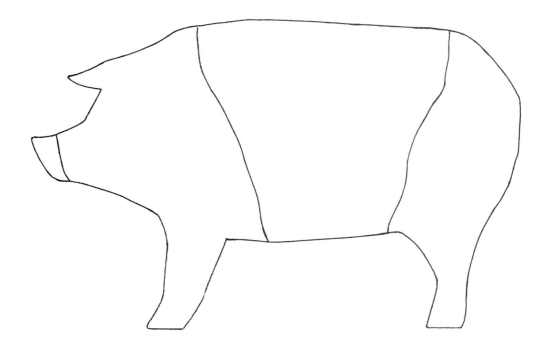

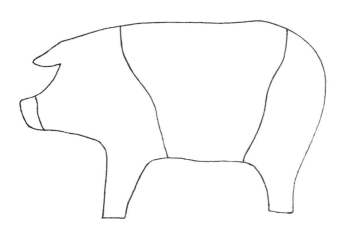

Illus. 66. Patterns and paint lines for pigs

Illus. 67. Patterns for sheep

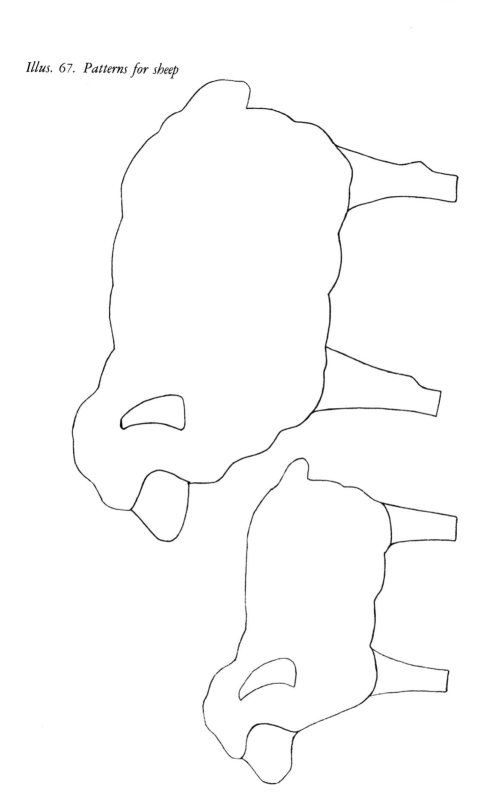

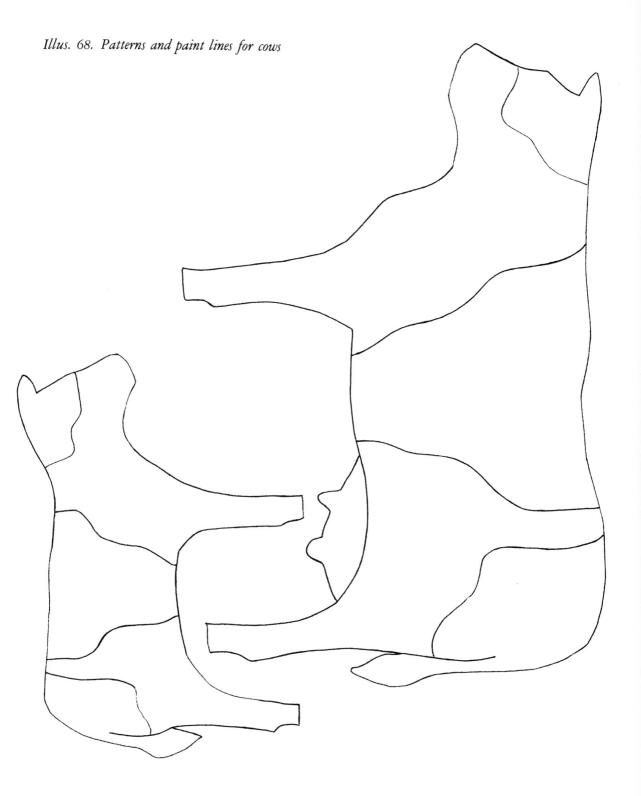

Illus. 68. Patterns and paint lines for cows

Illus. 69.

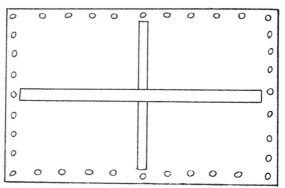

Illus. 70. Positions for gluing walls

Zoo

Any animal lover will cherish this toy. It is the perfect place to keep tiny toy animals or make a set of four wooden ones (see next chapter) to go with the set. Easy to make — fun to play with! Dowels can be removed easily for getting the animals in and out.

MATERIALS
Pine, ¾ in. thick: 9 × 24 in.
Pine, ⅜ in. thick: 10 × 12 in.
Wooden dowel, ⁵⁄₁₆ in. diameter: 20 ft. long
Acrylic paint: mars black, or substitute any color
Brush: 1 in.
Wood glue
Sandpaper: medium and fine grades
Tracing paper
Poster board

TOOLS
Band saw
Drill press (or drill) with ²¹⁄₆₄-in. bit

INSTRUCTIONS

Cutting. With the band saw, cut forty 5¾-in. lengths of ⁵⁄₁₆-in. dowel. Cut two 9 × 12-in. pieces of ¾-in. wood. From the ⅜-in. wood, cut one 4¼ × 10¼-in. piece and two 3½ × 4¼-in. pieces.

Drilling. Mark holes to be drilled on the top of one 9 × 12-in. board. There will be thirteen across the long side and nine down the short side. Holes are approximately ½ in. from the edge and ½ in. from each other. Adjust as necessary for evenness. Set this 9 × 12-in. board congruently on top of the other 9 × 12-in. board. If you have access to a drill press, I highly recommend using it to ensure straight and accurate holes.

Drill two corner holes first (through the top and ½ in. into the bottom board). Put a scrap piece of dowel in these holes to hold the boards in position. Now drill the remaining holes.

Sanding. Sand all pieces and round ends of dowels with medium-grade sandpaper. Give a final sanding to all pieces with fine sandpaper.

Gluing. Glue the walls to the bottom as shown in Illus. 70. Then glue the top in place, making sure holes are properly aligned. Let this dry before painting.

Painting. Paint entire zoo, except the dowels, with black paint or the color of your choice.

Assembling. For extra strength, glue the corner dowels in place. The rest of the dowels may be left unglued for easy play and animal removal. If you prefer, glue all front and back dowels, leaving only the side ones removable (Illus. 71).

For ease of carrying, you can make a rope handle. Drill four holes on top and thread two short lengths of rope through the holes, twisting them together before knotting ends.

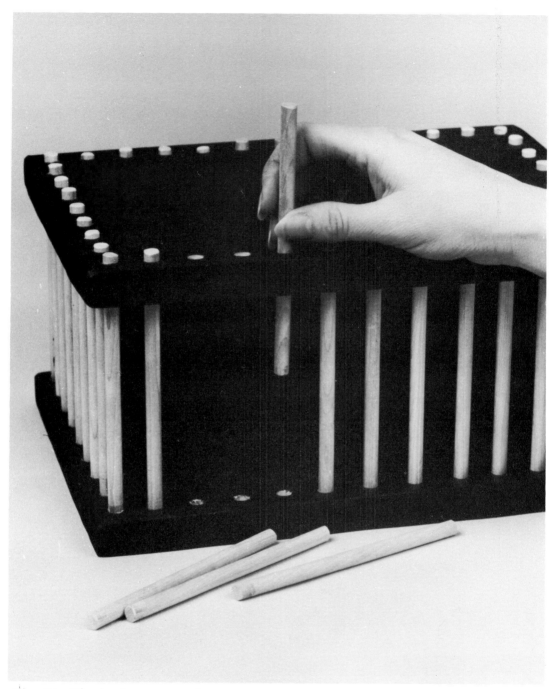

Illus. 71. The dowels are easy to insert or remove so that toys can be placed inside or taken outside of the cage.

Illus. 72.

Zoo Animals

A polar bear, a monkey, a cougar, and a seal—all waiting for a home in the zoo. These little animals, combined with the zoo, will provide hours of playtime. The animals are quick and easy to make.

MATERIALS
Pine, ¾ in. thick: 6 × 9 in.
Acrylic paint: titanium white, mars black, turner's yellow, naphthol red light, burnt umber

Brush: ½ in.
Sandpaper: medium and fine grades
Tracing paper
Poster board

TOOL
Scroll saw or band saw

INSTRUCTIONS

Pattern. Trace patterns and transfer onto poster board. Cut out this template and then trace figures onto the pine board.

Cutting. Cut out the animals with the scroll saw or band saw.

Illus. 73. Patterns for the polar bear, the seal, the cougar, and the monkey

Sanding. Sand each animal by hand with medium-grade sandpaper, making sure to sand well between legs, etc. Finish sanding with a fine-grade paper.

Painting. Paint the animals with the following mixtures. Measurements are approximate.
Polar bear: ½ tsp. white
Seal: ¼ tsp. white / ⅛ tsp. black
Monkey: ¼ tsp. yellow / ⅛ tsp. burnt umber

Cougar: ½ tsp. yellow / drop of red / drop of burnt umber
Eyes: paint a dot of white. When dry, paint a smaller dot of black on top of the white dot.

The animals are now ready to bed down in their new home—the zoo. For additional fun, make small wooden signs to use with the zoo (Illus. 74).

Illus. 74.

Rocking Toys

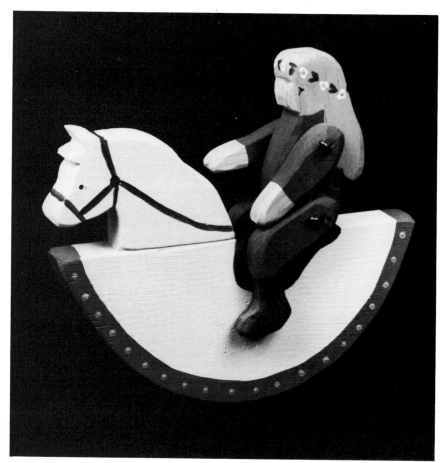

Illus. 75.

Rocking Horse & Rider

This adorable rocking horse, complete with rider, is not only charming to look at but also fun to play with. The girl is jointed and separate from the horse. They make a nice addition to any little girl's room.

MATERIALS
Pine, ¾ in. thick: 6 × 8 in.
Pine, ⅜ in. thick: 4 × 4 in.

Copper wire, 14 gauge: 6 in. long
Acrylic paint: titanium white, turner's yellow, cerulean blue hue, burnt umber, mars black, hooker's green
Brushes: ¼ in. and ½ in.
Wood glue
Sandpaper: medium and fine grades
Tracing paper
Poster board

TOOLS
Scroll saw or band saw
Drill with ³⁄₃₂-in. bit
Stationary belt sander or sanding wheel

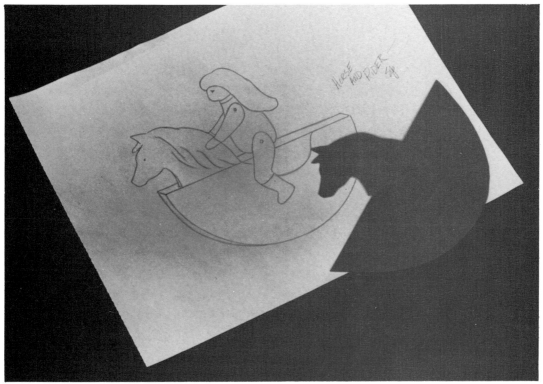

Illus. 76. Tracing the pattern

INSTRUCTIONS

Pattern. Trace pattern pieces and transfer onto poster board (Illus. 76). Cut out templates, cutting around outline only, and then trace horse's head, rocker, and girl's body onto the ¾-in. wood. Trace two arms and two legs onto the ⅜-in. wood.

Cutting. Cut out all pieces using either a scroll saw or band saw. Be extremely careful when cutting out small pieces so you don't injure yourself.

Drilling. Drill holes into the arms, legs, and body, as indicated, using the ³⁄₃₂-in. bit. Drill as straight as possible to ensure proper alignment of holes.

Sanding. Round edges of all pieces with the sander. The rounder the edge, the more carved it will look. Give a final sanding by hand with fine sandpaper.

Painting. Mix the approximate proportions of paint for the horse and rider. Horse: 1 tsp. white / drop of burnt umber Hair, decorative trim: ¼ tsp. yel-

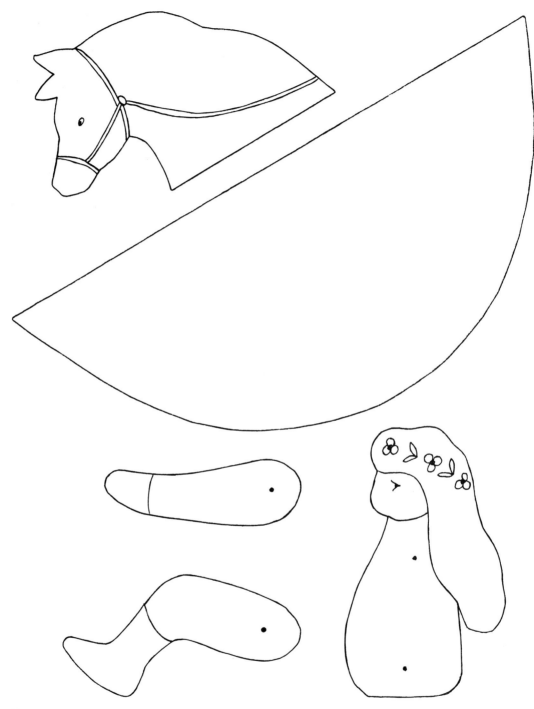

Illus. 77. Patterns for Rocking Horse & Rider

low / drop of burnt umber
Saddle, boots, reins: burnt umber
Clothing, trim: ¾ tsp. blue / ¼ tsp. white / ¼ tsp. black
Flowers: paint white flowers with yellow centers, green leaves
Eye: white dot / black dot on top of white dot

Assembling. Glue the horse's head in position as indicated in Illus. 75. Cut two 2½-in. lengths of wire and bend one end of each wire into a small closed oval, using the needle-nose pliers. Insert wire into arm, body, and other arm and bend end into another oval. Repeat this step with the legs.

Set the girl on her horse and she's ready to ride!

Rocking Rabbits

You can make these irresistible rabbits rock or remove them for creative play. A sure way to win someone's heart!

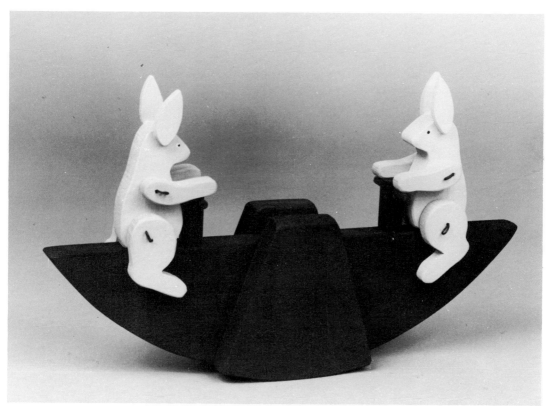

Illus. 78.

Illus. 79. Patterns for Rocking Rabbits

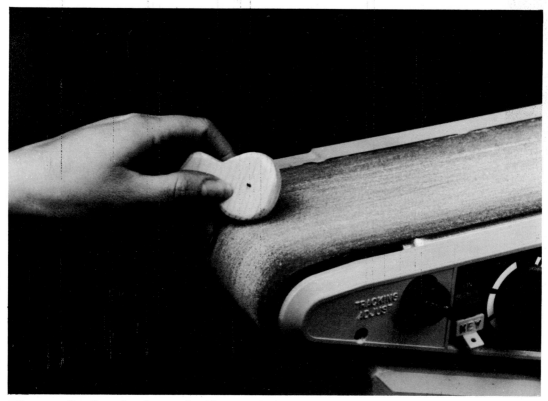

Illus. 80. Sanding the edges makes the pieces look carved and also removes sharp corners.

MATERIALS

Pine, ¾ in. thick: 6 × 14 in.
Pine, ⅜ in. thick: 3 × 5 in.
Birch plywood (or pine), ¼ in. thick: 2 × 2 in.
Wooden dowel, ³⁄₁₆ in. diameter: 4 in. long
Black steel wire, 16 gauge: 1 ft. long
Acrylic paint: titanium white, naphthol red light, mars black, cerulean blue hue, burnt umber
Brush: ½ in.
Sandpaper: medium and fine grades
Wood glue
Tracing paper
Poster board

TOOLS

Scroll saw or band saw
Drill with ³⁄₃₂-in. and ³⁄₁₆-in. bits
Stationary belt sander or sanding wheel
Needle-nose pliers

INSTRUCTIONS

Pattern. Trace pattern pieces and transfer onto poster board. Cut out poster-board patterns and then trace one large rocker piece, two small rocker pieces, and two rabbit bodies onto the ¾-in. wood. Trace patterns for four arms and four legs onto the ⅜-in. wood. Use the ¼-in. wood to trace four ears.

Cutting. Using the scroll saw or band saw, cut out all pattern pieces. Cut two small posts, ⅜ × 1¼ in., out of the ⅜-in. scraps. Then cut two 2-in. lengths of ³⁄₁₆-in.-diameter dowel.

Drilling. Drill holes, where indicated, into the arms, legs, and bodies using the ³⁄₃₂-in. bit. Using the ³⁄₁₆-in. bit, drill a hole into each post about ¼ in. from the top.

Sanding. Sand each piece so that the edges are rounded (Illus. 80). The arms and legs can be done using the sander, but be especially careful since they are rather difficult to hold onto. Sand the ears by hand and then finish sanding all pieces by hand using a fine-grade sandpaper.

Painting. Paint the pieces with the following color mixtures. Measurements are approximate.
All rabbit parts: 1 tsp. white / drop of burnt umber
Dowels, rocker supports: ½ tsp. blue / ⅛ tsp. white / ⅛ tsp. black
Large rocker, posts: 1½ tsp. red / drop of black
Eye: dot of white, dot of black on top of white dot

Assembling. Glue rocker supports to large rocker. Be sure rocking surfaces are smooth and even with one another. Glue posts to the top of the large rocker, approximately 3 in. from each end. Glue the rabbit ears in place. Insert dowels into the posts. Then cut four 2½-in. lengths of wire. Using the needle-nose pliers, bend one end of each wire until the end meets the wire. Insert a wire into an arm, through the rabbit's body, and then into the other arm. Curve this end around also. Repeat this procedure for remaining arms and legs. The arms and legs should be snug but still able to move.

Position rabbits on the rocker, with paws on the handle. Now they're ready for a rocking-good time!

Seesaw

These peppy penguins seesaw back and forth tirelessly once given a gentle start. A pendulum is the secret behind how this charming toy works.

MATERIALS
Pine, ¾ in. thick: 8 × 12 in.
Pine, ⅜ in. thick: 7 × 11 in.
Wooden dowel, ³⁄₁₆ in. diameter: two ½-in. lengths
Wooden dowel, ⁵⁄₁₆ in. diameter: 5½ in. long
Wooden dowel, ⅝ in. diameter: 4 in. long
Wooden dowel, ¾ in. diameter: two ¾-in. lengths
Round wood finial, 2 in. diameter
Black steel wire, 16 gauge: 1 ft. long
Acrylic paint: titanium white, mars black, turner's yellow, naphthol red light
Brush: ½ in.
Wood glue
Sandpaper: medium and fine grades
Tracing paper
Poster board

Illus. 81.

TOOLS

Scroll saw or band saw

Drill with ⅜-in., ³⁄₁₆-in., ⁵⁄₆₄-in., ⁷⁄₁₆-in., and ¹¹⁄₃₂-in. bits

Needle-nose pliers

INSTRUCTIONS

Pattern. Trace patterns and transfer them onto poster board. Cut out templates, cutting around the outlines only. Trace penguin bodies onto the ¾-in. wood. Then trace four wings, four legs, and two support pieces onto the ⅜-in. wood.

Cutting. Cut out all pieces with either a scroll saw or band saw. From the ¾-in. wood, cut a 3½ × 12-in. base piece. Also cut a 1 × 12-in. piece for the seesaw. Taper ends (Illus. 82). Cut dowels to measurements given on page 98.

Drilling. Drill ⁵⁄₆₄-in. holes into the penguin's body, wings, and legs, as indicated. Then drill an ¹¹⁄₃₂-in. hole into the middle of the seesaw to house the support dowel. Be sure the hole is as close to the center point as possible.

Illus. 82. This is the angle at which the seesaw ends should be tapered.

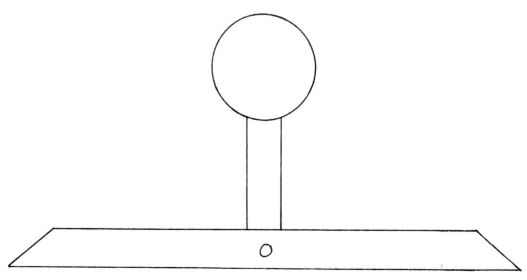

Illus. 83. Gluing position for pendulum

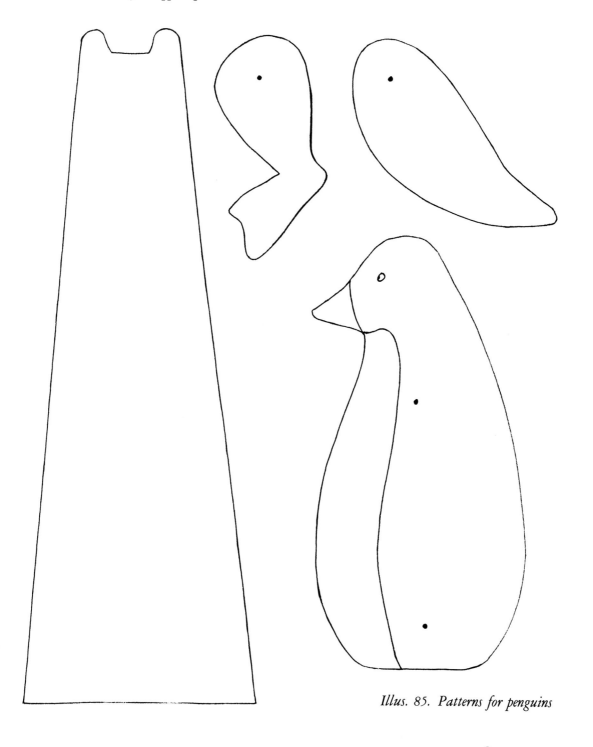

Illus. 84. Pattern for support pieces

Illus. 85. Patterns for penguins

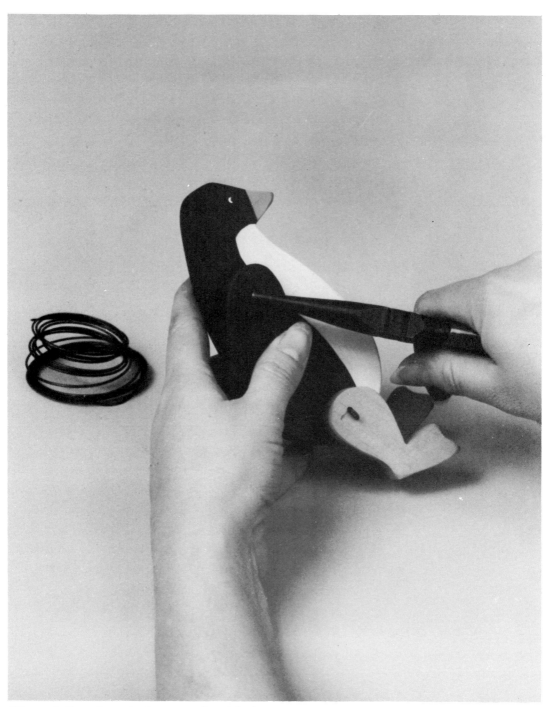

Illus. 86. Inserting wire into penguin with the pliers

Next, drill a hole halfway into the ¾-in.-diameter dowel pieces with the ⁵⁄₁₆-in. bit.

If the ball finial you are using does not have a hole large enough to fit the ⅝-in. dowel, drill halfway into the ball, using a ⅝-in. bit.

Sanding. Sand all pieces by hand with medium-grade sandpaper. Finish sanding with a fine-grade paper.

Painting. Draw paint lines as shown in Illus. 85. Paint pieces according to mixing instructions. Remember that measurements are approximate.
Penguin tummy, dowels, 2-in. ball: 1 tsp. white
Penguin, wings, dowel ends: 1 tsp. black
Seesaw: ½ tsp. red / drop of black
Base, supports, legs, beaks: 2 tsp. yellow / ¼ tsp. red
Eyes: paint a dot of white / paint a smaller dot of black on top of white dot

Assembling. Glue the base supports to the side of the base. Then glue the ⅝-in. dowel into the ball finial. When dry, glue the top of this dowel to the center bottom of the seesaw (Illus. 83). Let this dry well before moving.

Cut four lengths of steel wire approximately 2¾ in. long. Using the needle-nose pliers, turn one end of each wire into a small oval. Insert the straight end of the wire into one wing, through the body, and through the other wing. Turn the end of the wire (Illus. 86). Tighten against the body. Repeat this procedure with remaining wings and legs.

Slide the support dowel through the hole in the center of the seesaw. Glue the short ¾-in. dowel pieces onto the ends of the dowel. Set the seesaw on the base and test its moveability.

Now, the penguins may be glued in place or placed on the ⁵⁄₁₆-in. dowel pegs. Either way, you must now position the penguins in their *exact* balance point. Move them back and forth slightly until the seesaw stays level.

If gluing, glue the penguins in this position. If you choose to use dowels, as I did, mark the balance point under the center of each penguin. Drill a ⁵⁄₁₆-in. hole into the underside of each penguin about ¼ in. deep. Drill the corresponding holes in the seesaw. Insert and glue dowels into the seesaw. The penguins will be able to seesaw now without falling off, and yet they are still removable.

General Toys
&
Games

Illus. 87.

Illus. 88.

Blocks

Lettered blocks are a colorful and amusing introduction to the alphabet. They help develop not only reading skills, but also hand and eye coordination in very young children. You can make a child's name to display on their desk or you can send a block message for a special occasion (Illus. 88, 90).

MATERIALS
Small blocks: hardwood, 1½ × 1½ in.: any length
Large blocks: hardwood, 4 × 4 in.: any length
Block houses: hardwood, 2 × 4 in.: any length
Acrylic paint: assorted colors
Letter stencils
Stencil brushes
Sandpaper: medium and fine grades

TOOLS
Band saw: for small blocks, block houses
Saw, suitable for cutting 4 × 4's: for large blocks
Stationary belt sander

INSTRUCTIONS

Cutting. Cut selected wood into square blocks. For block houses (Color Illus. C1), cut various assorted sizes and then tilt the band-saw table to a 45° angle. Cut off both sides of the top approximately ¾ in. from the top (Illus. 89). Use scrap ¾-in. pieces for chimneys and cut off the bottom of these at the same angle.

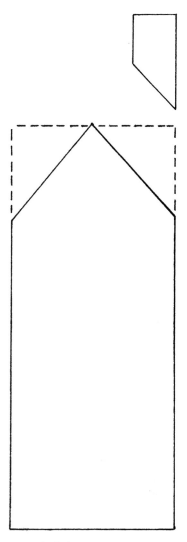

Illus. 89. Block house pattern and roof cuts

Sanding. Sand all edges and corners with the sander until a nice rounded edge has been achieved. Give each piece a final sanding by hand with fine-grade sandpaper.

Painting. The blocks may be painted many different colors and then stencilled,

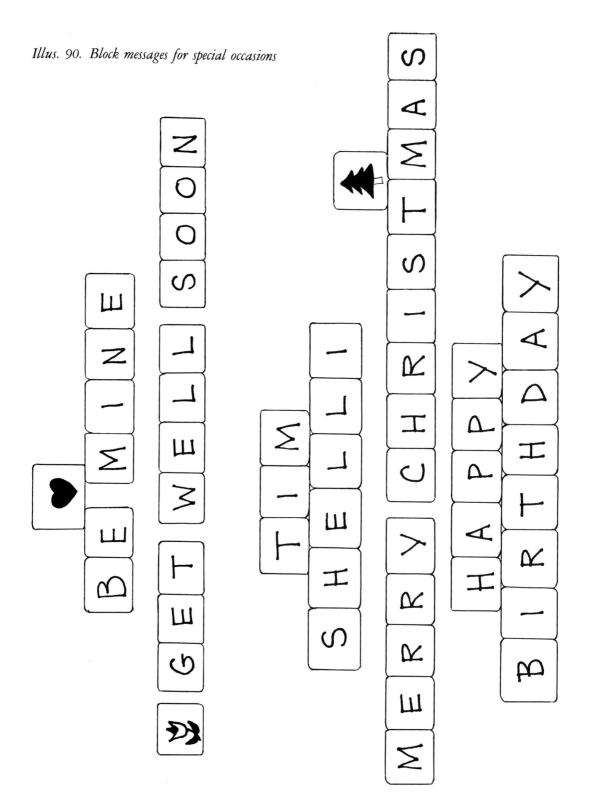

Illus. 90. Block messages for special occasions

or they may be left a natural color and stencilled.

Before painting the block houses, glue each roof into place. These houses may also be painted or left their natural color.

Stencilling. In the event that you have never stencilled before, here are some brief instructions.

When possible, tape the stencil into place with masking tape. This is rather difficult with small blocks, so hold the stencil flat against the block without moving it.

Dip the stencil brush into a small dab of paint. Work the paint into the brush by moving the brush in small circles against the surface the paint is on. On a paper towel, make small circular movements in various spots until your brush obviously has only a small amount of paint on the tip. Now, move the brush over the letter you are going to stencil in small circular motions until the letter is filled in (Illus. 91). Carefully lift the stencil straight up to avoid smearing. You will probably want to practice this on scrap wood first.

Stencil an assortment of letters and numbers or stencil a special message for a special occasion (Illus. 90). Print names on houses, such as BANK, HOTEL, STORE, and so on.

Illus. 91. Be sure to hold the stencil firmly against the wood so that you don't smear the edges.

Illus. 92.

Jointed Merry-Go-Round Animals

These miniature animals can be positioned walking, running, or leaping. Make a herd of one kind or make them all and arrange in an attractive grouping.

MATERIALS

Pine, ⅜ in. thick: 11 × 24 in.
Pine, ¾ in. thick: 5 × 15 in.
Birch plywood, ¼ in. thick: 2 × 2 in. (rabbit ears)
Wooden dowel, ³⁄₁₆ in. diameter: 25 in. long
Wooden dowel, ⅛ in. diameter: 15 in. long
Acrylic paint: titanium white, mars black, burnt umber, naphthol red light, turner's yellow, cerulean blue hue, permanent green deep
Brushes: ¼ in. and ½ in.
Stain: medium color

Wood glue
Sandpaper: medium and fine grades
Tracing paper
Poster board

TOOLS

Scroll saw or band saw
Drill with ⅛-in. and ³⁄₁₆-in. bits
Stationary belt sander or sanding wheel
Small hammer

INSTRUCTIONS

Pattern. Trace all pattern pieces and transfer onto poster board. Cut out these templates around the outline and then trace one body, two front and two hind legs for each animal onto the ⅜-in. wood. Also trace the reindeer antlers. Trace two rabbit ears onto the ¼-in. wood.

Cutting. Using a scroll saw or band saw, cut out the above pieces and then, from the ¾-in. wood, cut five bases, 2¼ × 4½ in. Cut two 4-in. lengths and three 5-in. lengths of the ³⁄₁₆-in. dowel. Animals will be staggered in height. Also cut a 1½-in. length for the unicorn's horn. From the ⅛-in. dowel, cut twenty ¾-in. pieces. These will be for the joints.

Drilling. With the ⅛-in. bit, drill holes into each leg and body as marked on the

Illus. 93.

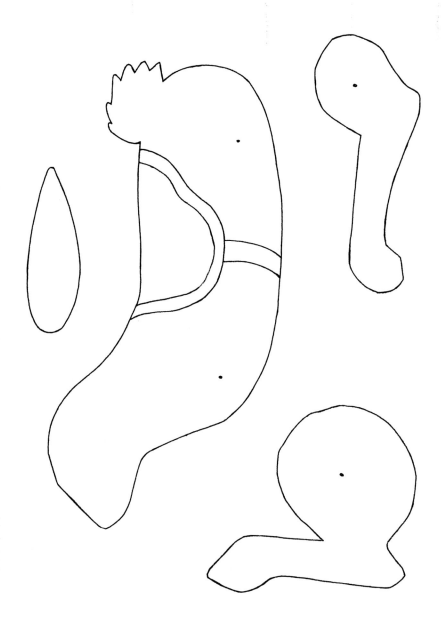

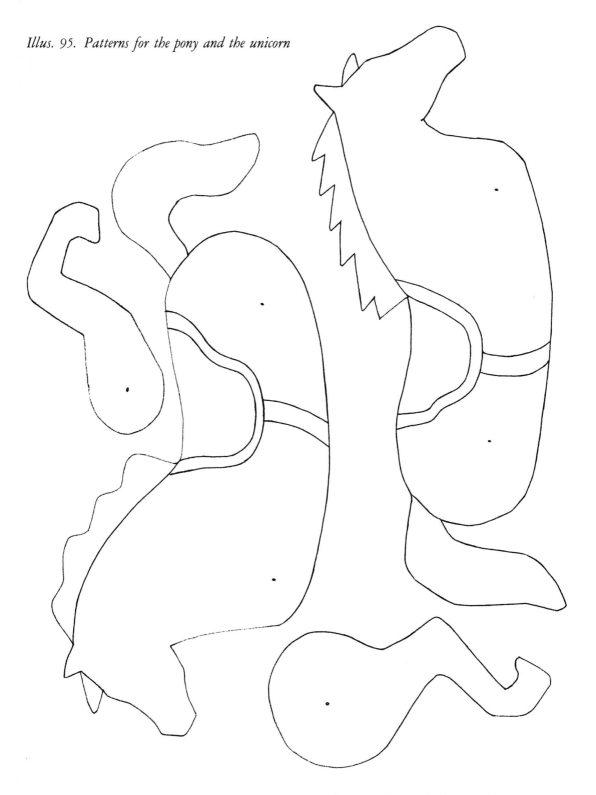

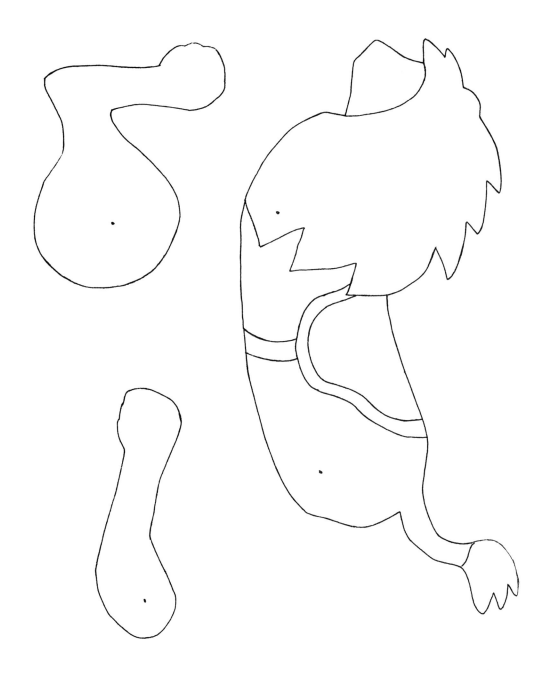

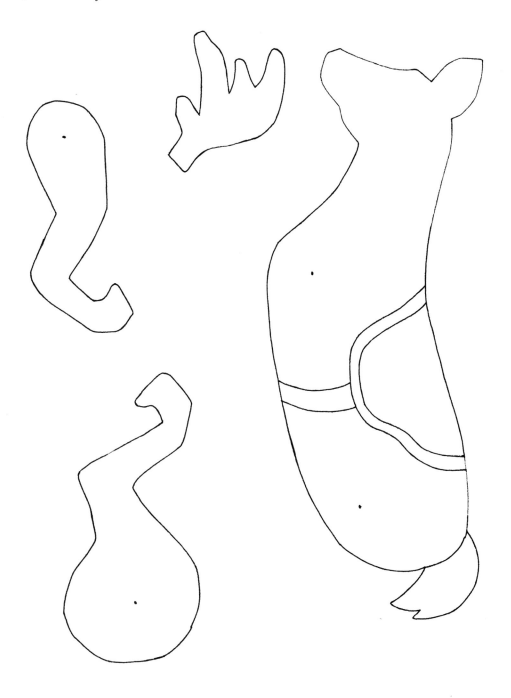

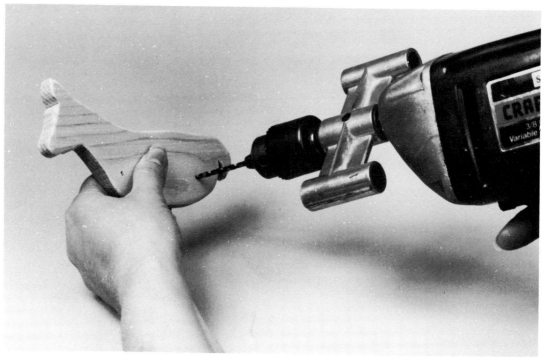

Illus. 98. When drilling into the wood, be sure the angle is perpendicular to the surface.

pattern (Illus. 98). Then, using the ³/₁₆-in. bit, drill a hole approximately ½ in. in depth into the underside of each animal and also into the center of each base. Use this bit to drill a hole into the forehead of the unicorn for his horn.

Sanding. Sand the edges of all body pieces and legs until rounded. This will give a carved appearance. Sand the bases and then sand the small ³/₁₆-in. dowel to a tapered point.

Give each piece a final sanding with a fine-grade paper.

Staining. Stain each base piece with a medium-color stain. Set these aside to dry.

Painting. Paint the animals with the paint mixtures below. Measurements are approximate (see Illus. 99 for point lines).

Rabbit and unicorn bodies, legs, pony's mane, tail: 1 tsp. white / drop of burnt umber

Pony body, legs: ¼ tsp. white / ¼ tsp. black

Reindeer body, legs: ¼ tsp. white / ¼ tsp. burnt umber

Reindeer antlers, tail: ⅛ tsp. white / ¹/₁₆ tsp. burnt umber

Lion body, legs, unicorn horn: ½ tsp. yellow / few drops burnt umber

Lion mane, tail: ⅛ tsp. burnt umber

Unicorn mane, tail: ⅛ tsp. white / drop of black

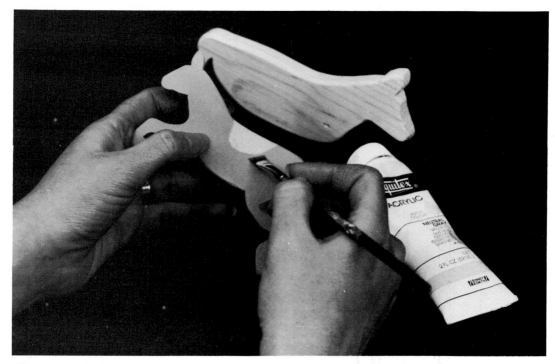

Illus. 99. Painting

Saddles and cinches: ½ tsp. red / drop of black

Saddle trim: rabbit and lion, blue; unicorn, green; reindeer, yellow; pony, black

Assembling. Using a small hammer, tap a dowel into each leg until only ⅛ in. is extending on the top surface. Insert the other end into the body of the corresponding animal. The legs should move easily, but should not be too loose.

Glue the horn into the unicorn's forehead. Also glue on the reindeer's antler and rabbit's ears.

Insert the 3/16-in. dowels into the bases and set the animals on top for display. Since these animals are jointed they can be positioned in many ways or played with when removed from the dowel.

Wagon

Whether it is the capacity to contain toys or the ability to roll them into a favorite playing spot, wagons have proved their efficiency and mobility to children for hundreds of years. This one has been designated for bears only, but you could,

Illus. 100.

of course, inscribe the side with any word—a name, a place, or a slogan—or perhaps with numbers. This wagon can hold fifty-six small wooden blocks and could be designated a BLOCK wagon.

MATERIALS
Pine, ¾ in. thick: 8 × 14 in.
Pine, ⅜ in. thick: 3 × 12 in.
Birch plywood, ¼ in. thick: 8¼ × 12 in.
Wooden dowel, ³⁄₁₆ in. diameter: 30 in. long
Cotter pins, ³⁄₁₆ × ½: four
Flat wood screw

Acrylic paint: naphthol red light, burnt umber
Brush: 1 in.
Letter stencils
Stencil brush
Wood glue
Sandpaper: medium and fine grades
Tracing paper
Poster board

TOOLS
Band saw
Drill with ⅟₁₆-in., ³⁄₁₆-in., and ¹³⁄₆₄-in. bits
Circle-cutting bit, 2¼ in. diameter
Screwdriver

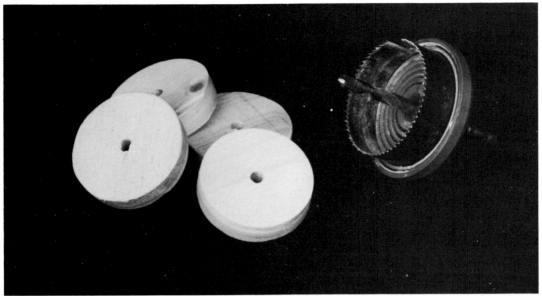

Illus. 101. A circle-cutting bit makes smooth wheels very quickly.

INSTRUCTIONS

Pattern. Trace patterns for the axle support and handle support and transfer onto poster board. Cut these out and then trace the handle support onto the ⅜-in. wood. Also draw a ¾ × 9-in. handle on this wood. On the ¾-in. wood, trace four axle supports.

Cutting. Cut out the above pieces plus two 2¼ × 6¾-in. pieces and two 2¼ × 12-in. pieces from ¾-in. wood. Leave space for four 2¼-in. wheels that will be drilled out.

Also cut a bottom, 8¼ × 12 in., from the ¼-in. wood. Cut two 10½-in. lengths of

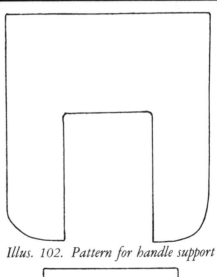

Illus. 102. Pattern for handle support

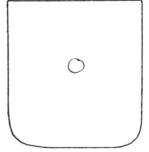

Illus. 103. Pattern for axle supports: cut four.

dowel and also a 2⅛-in. and a 2½-in. length.

Drilling. From the ¾-in. wood, drill out four 2¼-in. wheels with the circle-cutting bit (Illus. 101). Use the ¹³⁄₆₄-in. bit to drill through the middle of each wheel.

Using the ³⁄₁₆-in. bit, drill through the middle of the axle supports and also through the top of the handle as shown in Illus. 100.

Hold the other end of the handle in the support slot and drill sideways through all three thicknesses. Using the ¹⁄₁₆-in. bit, drill through both ends of axle dowels to hold the cotter pins (Illus. 104).

Illus. 104. Points at which holes should be drilled in ends of dowel.

Sanding. Sand all pieces well with medium-grade sandpaper. Finish sanding with a fine-grade paper.

Gluing. Glue and clamp sides to front and back. Glue bottom in place and then glue axle supports flush with the sides and about 1½ in. from front and back.

Painting. Paint the wagon with watered-down naphthol red light (use only about 1½ tsp. of paint). Then paint handle and wheels with watered-down burnt umber (about 1½ tsp.).

Stencil desired name or words on the side.

See stencilling instructions on page 109. Apply any color desired.

Assembling. Slide the 2⅛-in. dowel through the handle support and attach handle. Insert and glue dowel handle into top of handle section. Screw the handle support to the wagon. Leave loose enough for movement.

Insert the axle dowels and then slide on wheels. Fasten cotter pins, and this wagon is ready to roll!

Doll Cradle

This is a replica of an antique doll cradle, a perfect home for any doll or bear. Although this cradle was finished in a dark color, it would also be attractive if painted a colonial blue or antique red.

MATERIALS
Pine, ¾ in. thick: 1¾ × 8 in.
Pine, ⅜ in. thick: 10 × 34 in.
Acrylic paint: burnt umber, naphthol red light
Brush: 1 in.
Wood glue
Sandpaper: medium and fine grades
Tracing paper
Poster board

TOOLS
Scroll saw or band saw
Stationary belt sander or sanding wheel

Illus. 105.

INSTRUCTIONS

Pattern. Trace all pattern pieces and transfer them onto poster board. Cut out these templates and then trace onto the ⅜-in. wood. Trace two sides and two rockers. Also draw out a 5½ × 12-in. bottom piece.

Cutting. Cut out the above pieces and also cut a 1¾ × 8-in. support piece from the ¾-in. wood. This will be glued to the bottom between the rockers for extra support.

Sanding. Sand all pieces with the sander. Round the rocker tips and all top edges of the cradle.

Because the bottom edges of the front and back must recline at an angle, sand them so that they fit flush with the bottom.

Give each piece a final sanding by hand, using a fine-grade sandpaper.

Gluing. Glue and clamp the front and back to the sides. Then glue the bottom in place. Center the bottom support and glue to the bottom. Position the rockers, gluing them to both the support and the bottom.

Painting. Mix approximately 1 tsp. burnt umber with 1 tsp. red. Paint the entire cradle this color.

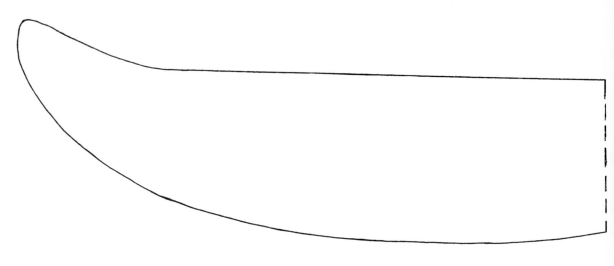

Illus. 106. Pattern for rockers

Illus. 107. Pattern for cradle sides

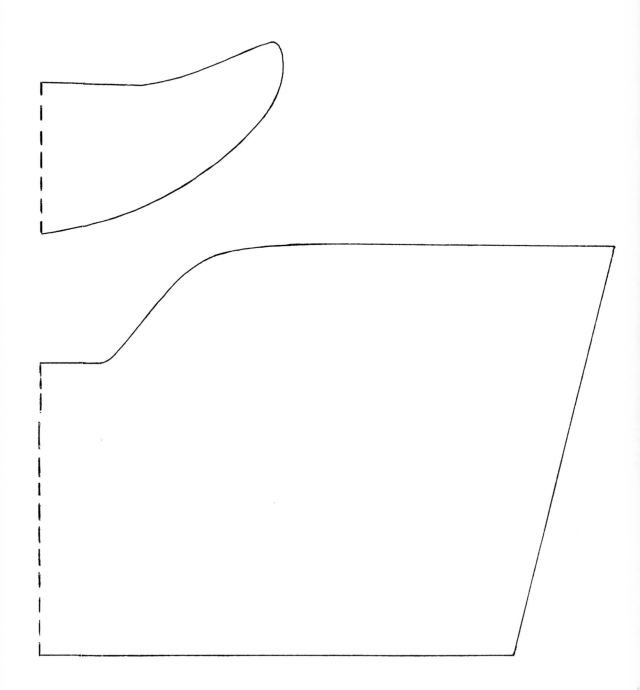

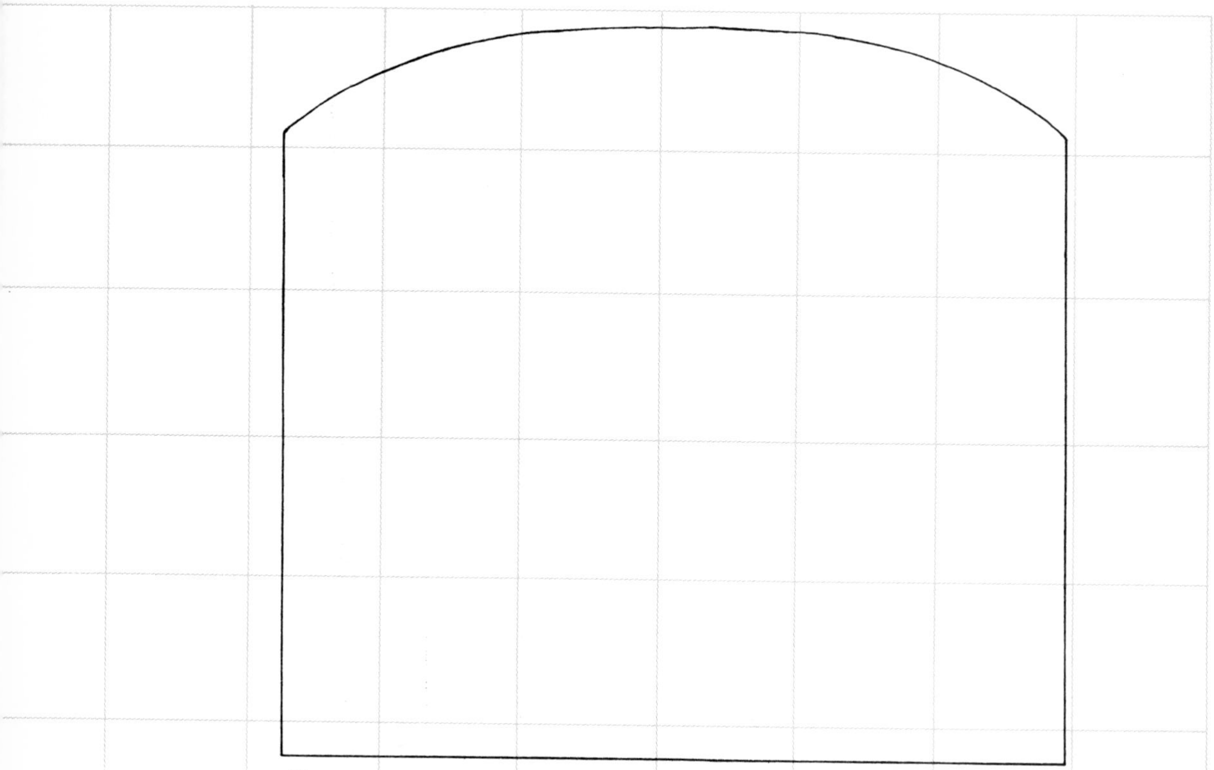

Illus. 108. Pattern for headboard

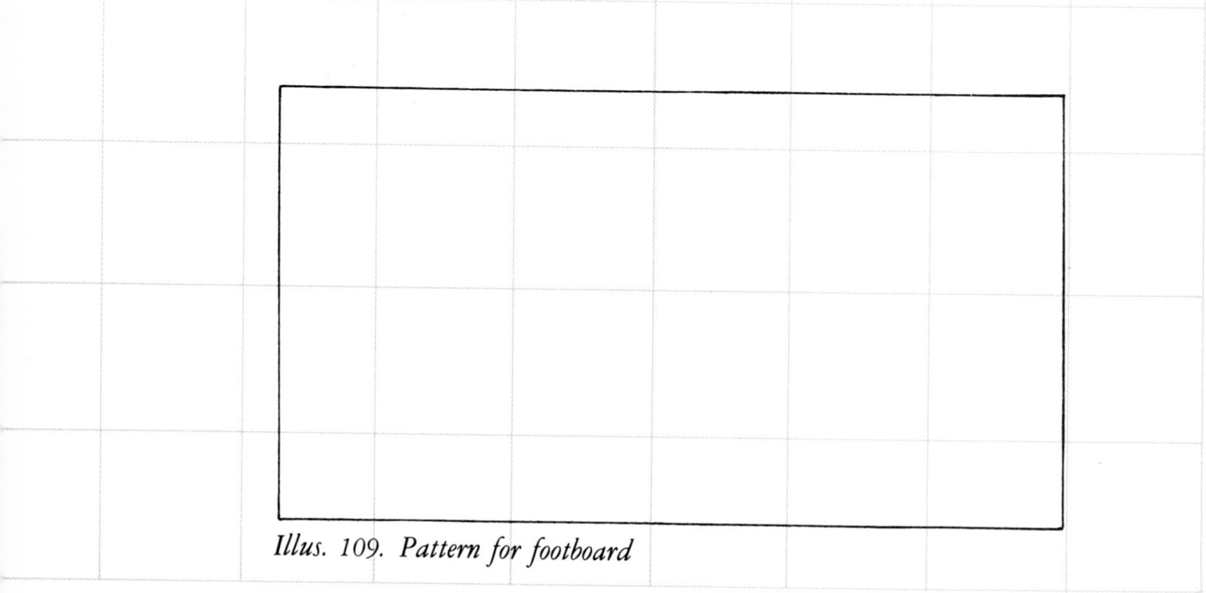

Illus. 109. Pattern for footboard

Illus. 110.

Checkerboard & Checkers

Checkers, or draughts, is a board game dating back to ancient times. This simple-to-make game can provide hours of enjoyment for the entire family. Charming to look at, the game can be on display continuously for spur-of-the-moment play.

MATERIALS

Pine, ¾ in. thick: 11 × 15 in.
Wooden dowel, ¾ in. diameter: 1 ft. long
Acrylic paint: titanium white, mars black
Brush: stencil or regular
Checkerboard stencil (optional): 1 in. squares
Stain: light oak
Semigloss lacquer
Sandpaper: medium and fine grades

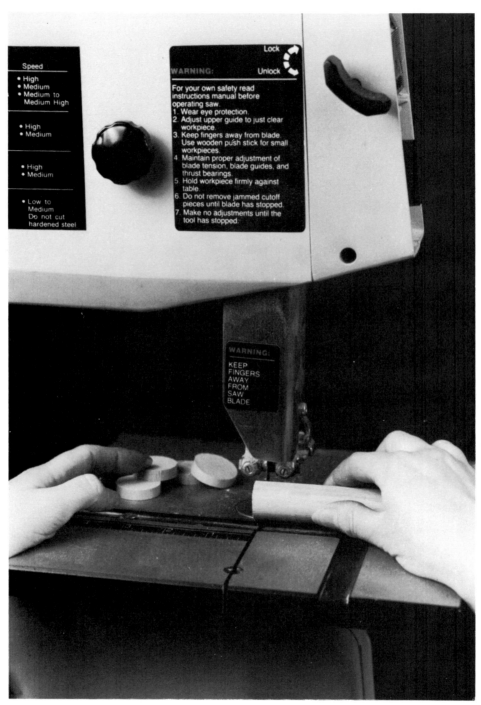

Illus. 111. Cutting checkers from a dowel is easy on this saw.

TOOL
Band saw

INSTRUCTIONS

Cutting. Cut a ¾-in.-thick board 11 × 15 in. Then cut twenty-four ¼-in. slices of the ¾-in. dowel (Illus. 111).

Sanding. Sand all edges well. Round the top edges of the board either by hand or with a sander, using medium-grade sandpaper.

Remember to sand with the grain of the wood. Give each piece a final sanding by hand with a fine-grade paper.

Painting and Staining. Paint twelve checkers white and twelve checkers black, or apply traditional colors of red and black.

If you have chosen to stencil your checkerboard, see stencilling instructions on page 109. If you are hand painting, draw eight 1-in. squares across and eight down. Make sure your grid is centered on the board. Paint alternate squares of white and black.

When the paint has dried, apply to the board a light oak stain. Wipe off any excess. When dry, seal with a coat of semi-gloss lacquer.

INDEX